BE A NETWORK
MARKETING LEADER

BE A NETWORK MARKETING LEADER

Build a Community to Build Your Empire

Mary Christensen

△MACOM

American Management Association

New York • Atlanta • Brussels • Chicago • Mexico City
San Francisco • Shanghai • Tokyo • Toronto • Washington, D.C.

Bulk discounts available. For details visit:
www.amacombooks.org/go/specialsales
Or contact special sales:
Phone: 800-250-5308
Email: specialsls@amanet.org
View all the AMACOM titles at: www.amacombooks.org
American Management Association: www.amanet.org

This publication is designed to provide accurate and authoritative information in regard to the subject matter covered. It is sold with the understanding that the publisher is not engaged in rendering legal, accounting, or other professional service. If legal advice or other expert assistance is required, the services of a competent professional person should be sought.

Library of Congress Cataloging-in-Publication Data
Christensen, Mary, 1951-
 Be a network marketing leader : build a community to build your empire / Mary Christensen.
  pages cm
 Includes index.
 ISBN 978-0-8144-3682-0 (pbk.) — ISBN 978-0-8144-3683-7 (ebook) 1. Multi-level marketing. 2. Direct marketing. I. Title.
 HF5415.126.C4877 2016
 658.8'72—dc23   2015029950

About AMA
American Management Association (www.amanet.org) is a world leader in talent development, advancing the skills of individuals to drive business success. Our mission is to support the goals of individuals and organizations through a complete range of products and services, including classroom and virtual seminars, webcasts, webinars, podcasts, conferences, corporate and government solutions, business books, and research. AMA's approach to improving performance combines experiential learning—learning through doing—with opportunities for ongoing professional growth at every step of one's career journey.

Printing number
10 9 8 7 6 5 4 3 2 1

This book is dedicated to the people I love the most.
Thank you **Nikki**, **David**, **Wayne**, **Samantha**,
Brayden, **Paige**, **Trinity**, and **Jett** for being in my life.
I feel as though I have the best family in the world.

Contents

Part Three
Learn to Communicate

Part Four
Leading Your Team

Part Five
Going Forward

Acknowledgments

Grateful thanks to these highly respected network marketing leaders for their generous contributions to this book: Cindy and Scott Monroe, founders, Thirty-One Gifts, LLC; Renée Hornbaker, CFO, Stream Energy; Bob Hipple, CEO, Damsel in Defense; Dr. Traci Lynn, founder, Traci Lynn Jewelry; Tom and Kelly Gaines, founders, Pink Zebra Home; Jessica Kim, president, Barefoot Books; Jim Lupkin and Brian Carter, authors, *Network Marketing for Facebook*; and Karen Clark, owner, My Business Presence.

And, as always, thank you to Ellen Kadin, executive editor, and Therese Mausser, director of International Rights and Sales, at AMACOM Books, for your continuing support and encouragement.

BE A NETWORK MARKETING LEADER

It's All in Your Hands

One of the greatest achievements you can realize is to live a life without financial constraints. Financial freedom gives you choices. You can choose where you live and how you live, how you'll raise your children and spend your leisure time. You can make a difference by supporting a global charity or giving back to your local community. When your horizons open, the world becomes your oyster.

Most people sacrifice financial freedom for security. They play it safe, settling for a *forty-forty* existence, working forty hours a week to earn $40,000 a year. Because they shy away from risk, they never discover what their lives could have been.

If you're playing it safe because you are willing to let your fears limit you, or others dictate how you live, this book is not for you. You must be willing to extend the walls of your comfort zone before you can grow to fill the space.

If you want the lifestyle financial freedom brings, and you're willing to work for it, I can show you how to achieve financial freedom by building your own network marketing empire.

Network marketing is the ideal business for anyone with big dreams and the courage to pursue them. From the moment you sign an independent contractor agreement with the company you choose to partner with, you become CEO of your own start-up. You hold the key to your destiny in your own hands.

> When you love what you do it's not a job,
> it's a lifestyle.

Network marketing can be summed up in one word: *opportunity*. There are no guarantees of financial freedom. It takes determination, discipline, and drive to reach the highest incomes. Those traits are written into your DNA. Most of us are descended from pioneers who crossed oceans and continents seeking a better life.

Every person who blazes a trail opens a new path for others to follow, and millions have traveled the network marketing route to financial and lifestyle freedom. Each of them has smoothed the way for you to pursue your dreams. But no one gets an express pass. Everyone has to travel the same route. As is true with any endeavor, the more you put into it, the more you'll get out of it.

If you are ambitious, hardworking, and determined, you'll succeed at almost any path you choose in life. What attracts entrepreneurs to network marketing is that you won't be competing against others to reach the highest incomes. You'll be competing for yourself. It's your race and you'll set the pace.

You'll decide when you work, where you work, and how you work. If you're not getting the results you want, you won't have to consult with a committee or gain approval from a supervisor before trying something new. You will call the shots on the direction your business takes and the strategies you employ.

By the time I discovered network marketing I'd already been through a dysfunctional childhood and a failed marriage. It wasn't an auspicious start, but a voice inside me always said: *You deserve better than this.*

The turning point in my life was becoming the sole provider for my children. They gave me the motivation to stop hoping for a better life, and the willpower to start creating it.

My network marketing journey started with such a small step I never imagined how far it would take me. I saw an advertisement that offered work from home, and I picked up the phone. Within hours I had purchased my starter kit and, although I didn't see it at the time, started my journey to financial freedom.

I first saw network marketing as a temporary job that would pay the bills until my children were old enough to allow me to return to my teaching job. When I started earning more in my business than I earned as a teacher, I realized I didn't have to depend on someone else for my income. It was a huge eye-opener, and cemented my belief in the potential of network marketing.

It was no walk in the park, and my fears didn't dissolve overnight, but timidity has never been one of my faults. When you grow up in the war zone created by an abusive, alcoholic father, you can't afford the luxury of faintheartedness. You grow strong to survive.

That I meet many successful network marketers who are succeeding despite major trauma in their lives is proof that no one has to settle for less because of a few challenges, or let their current circumstances determine their future circumstances. We don't all get a smooth ride, but locking ourselves into a victim mindset won't get us out of a mess. The only way out is action.

When you're ready to throw off the straitjacket of self-doubt, you'll discover that most setbacks are temporary. It's only when you give up that they become permanent. When you're ready to define yourself by your strengths and not your shortcomings, you'll discover that you don't need confidence to achieve financial freedom. You need courage. Courage will help you block out your doubts, push through your barriers, and keep advancing no matter how many missteps you make, or falls you take.

I know God won't give me anything I can't handle.
I just wish he didn't trust me so much.
MOTHER TERESA

No one is more deserving, or has a better chance of financial freedom than you. You may come from a tiny town, have left college before you graduated, or be the first in your family to break free. You may have struggles to overcome and skills to master. Don't let that stop you.

It's not where you start in life that defines you.
It's where you go.

With only four and a half million people, my birth country of New Zealand is a tiny nation. But it was founded by, and has always been recognized as, a nation of strivers, starting with the first settlers who landed on the isolated islands to forge a new life.

New Zealand was the first country in the world to give women the right to vote. The first person to conquer the world's highest mountain was a New Zealander. One of the greatest sports teams in the world, the mighty All Blacks rugby team, comes from New Zealand. They're world champions because they have the determination, discipline, and drive to succeed.

When you give yourself permission to succeed you'll see challenges as opportunities and you'll tackle them head-on. You won't look back, you won't make excuses, and you won't give in. You'll live by the creed *I succeed or I learn.*

The only way to fail is to quit before you succeed.

The toughest battle you'll fight to become a network marketing leader will be inside your own head. Win that battle and you'll be free to start pursuing your dreams.

You won't be taking the journey alone. If it were a country, network marketing would be the thirteenth largest by population in the world. According to the most recent data from the World Federation of Direct Selling Associations (WFDSA), more than 96 million independent contractors currently work a network marketing business.

The overwhelming majority of network marketers are doing it for small change. But don't let the statistics deter you. Most network marketers choose to work their businesses on a casual basis. Some join to buy their favorite products wholesale, and others to make a few dollars selling them to family and friends. Many become network marketers for the social, intellectual, and emotional benefits the experience provides.

If your goal is financial freedom you can achieve it if you are willing to adopt the attitudes and attributes of a leader:

- Courage to set an ambitious goal
- Determination to pursue it vigorously
- Motivation to work even when you don't feel like it
- Discipline to block out doubts, distractions, and detractors
- Strength to push beyond your former achievements
- Maturity to take responsibility for everything that happens
- Willingness to work on your weaknesses
- Empathy to build lasting relationships
- Resolve to take on a leadership role
- Stamina to keep going when the going gets tough

You won't have to jettison your job or abandon your studies to build your business. Even working part-time or flexible hours (by which I don't mean optional hours) you can make significant progress over time.

This book is based on my own personal experiences building successful network marketing businesses and helping others do the same. Some of the most highly respected leaders in the industry have generously contributed their advice and perspectives. Collectively we have helped millions of network marketers succeed.

Now it's your turn to build a network marketing empire by creating a community where people are eager to work, encouraged to learn, and excited to grow.

PART **ONE**

Ready to Lead

CHAPTER 1

The Power of Network Marketing

It has never been easier to take an entrepreneurial approach to financial freedom. Seismic advances in technology have abolished all barriers to working from home, and network marketing has expanded into almost every product and service imaginable.

Network marketing is the ultimate opportunity for entrepreneurs. The traditional wellness, personal care, fashion accessories, home care, and food sectors are thriving, and the products available through network marketing channels are increasingly innovative. You can build a business around personalized health coaching, custom jewelry, gourmet foods, gift baskets, and personal defense products.

Network marketing has become a key player in the delivery of services. Your business could be based on energy, insurance, credit monitoring, legal services, home security, or telecommunications. Whatever product, service, or channel appeals to you, you'll find a network marketing corporation eager to partner with you, and a sponsor willing to mentor you.

The core of network marketing is selling products and services person-to-person. It's the perfect business in our consumer-driven society.

Network marketers don't have a monopoly on supplying products and services, but they do have an advantage. In today's highly connected marketplace, consumers actively seek recommendations from someone whose opinion they can trust. That person is not an overworked sales assistant earning minimum wage. Consumers want the convenience of seven-days-a-week, twenty-four-hours-a-day online shopping, and the support of a person who has a vested interest in satisfying their needs when they need help or advice. That person can be you.

According to a Harris Poll commissioned by the World Federation of Direct Selling Associations (WFDSA) one in three adults in the United States purchased from a direct seller in the previous six months.

As a network marketer, there is no limit on where you can go to find and service your customers. You can market your products online, face-to-face, or a combination of both. Your online store never closes, and you are always one message, text, or call away from your customers.

Selling products and services is only the start of network marketing's appeal. In addition to the profit you will make on your personal sales, you will earn bonuses on your "organizational" sales (the sales of the people you sponsor and the sales of the people they sponsor).

All network marketers start their business by signing an independent contractor agreement with their chosen corporate partner. Although the contract is with the company, they become part of the organization of the person who sponsors them.

The company remunerates leaders who introduce and mentor others by paying them bonuses on their organizational sales.

Although compensation plans vary from company to company, they are all designed to reward growth. The more skilled you are at attracting and mentoring others to successfully build businesses, the more money you'll make. Specifics of how your company remunerates independent contractors will be clearly laid out in its compensation plan.

· ·

The concept of getting what you want in life by helping others get what they want is not new. Almost a century has passed since John Rockefeller is said to have declared "I'd rather earn 1 percent of 100 people's efforts than 100 percent of my own efforts."

What's new is that mobile devices have changed the game. You can work from home, your car, or your favorite coffee shop. You can build a network marketing organization in your hometown, or another state, or another country. If your corporate partner has a global compensation plan you can build your business on another continent.

When you travel, your business will travel with you. You can run your business while you're waiting to board your flight to an exciting destination, or enjoying family time at a theme park.

Network marketing is the original social network. Facebook COO Sheryl Sandberg acknowledged it by telling the audience at the 2014 Congress of the WFDSA: "Direct Sellers mastered personalized marketing before Facebook even existed, and we've learned a lot from the way direct sellers have always run their businesses."

That's why network marketing is the "It" industry for today's aspiring entrepreneurs. Flexibility, fun, and freedom are part of the package. Personal growth is practically guaranteed. It's almost impossible to grow a network marketing business without growing yourself.

••

Warren Buffett, the most successful business investor of our times and one of the world's wealthiest men, is the largest shareholder of investment group Berkshire Hathaway Group, which owns a network marketing company.

••

One of the many reasons for network marketing's current rise in popularity is that our concept of the ideal lifestyle has evolved. With a connection to the world at our fingertips we're seeking ways to blend our personal and business lives.

When we work from home, we don't feel the need to separate our family and business lives. We have the best of both worlds. We have the money, and the freedom to enjoy it. Fifty-five percent of European workers rank work/life balance as their number one career aspiration, and enjoyment and happiness are more important than earnings, according to a Global Career Aspiration survey published by Right Management.

A network marketing business is the perfect model of work/play integration. As CEO of your own business you won't be chained to a desk or spending your day with people you wouldn't choose as friends. You'll decide with whom you'll work, associate, and play.

You can pursue your degree, or keep your full-time job while you're building your business. Network marketing leaders often set out with a goal to replace their full-time income, and many achieve it. They're living proof that the business works . . . *if you do*!

Network marketing is attracting the attention of high-flying corporate employees who are now rethinking their options. Many no longer want to sacrifice their personal lives to work for a corporation that could replace them without warning or conscience. Not only do they have the skills to build a successful business, they have the motivation to do it.

> The price of anything is the amount of life
> you exchange for it.
> HENRY DAVID THOREAU

Stand-alone business owners are waking up to the appeal of network marketing. They've always worked long hours to make a modest profit, and the risk they take borders on the ridiculous.

What makes network marketing an attractive alternative is that you won't have to cash out your savings, go cap in hand to the bank, or seek crowdfunding to start your business.

According to Bloomberg, a respected source of global business and financial information, eight out of ten new businesses fail within the first eighteen months. A network marketing business typically costs a few hundred dollars or less. If you decide it's not for you, you can leave with your assets intact.

Most network marketing starter kits come with products and business supplies worth many times the cost of your investment. Many corporations include a three- to twelve-month subscription to a highly sophisticated online store and virtual office website free with the starter kit. After that you will pay only a nominal amount for the company to maintain your cyber office and store for you.

The corporation you partner with will cover most of your start-up costs, and you can cover ongoing expenses from the profits you make. You'll also be able to take advantage of the significant tax breaks that are available to home-based entrepreneurs.

Always seek the advice of a tax professional, preferably one who specializes in small and/or home-based businesses for what expenses you can claim.

In households where both parents are working by necessity, not choice, a network marketing business is the perfect way to fill the gap between the family's financial obligations and its income.

One of the many reasons network marketing is thriving is that no one is buying the job security message anymore. Manufacturing, distribution, and service jobs are evaporating as corporations automate the functions people used to perform. The world's largest online retailer added 10,000 robots to its distribution warehouse in one year. Faster, more efficient dispatching and delivery of orders is a plus for customers, but it comes at the cost of thousands of jobs going up in smoke.

We're booking our appointments online and ordering our food from a tablet at our table. We're checking ourselves onto our flights and into our hotel rooms. For the millions who worked in the service industry the American dream is skirting close to a nightmare.

Ask any worker if he or she enjoys the uncertainty of keeping a job, the daily commute, the measly vacation and sick day allowances, or being asked to work overtime and then being told, "We can't afford to give you a pay raise this year." Most will say: "I can't wait to get out of here!"

Ask parents if they want to put their kids in day care eight to ten hours a day. Many will give you an audience when you offer to show them how to be home with their kids and build a profitable business at the same time.

Many millennials grew up in homes that bore the brunt of the last global recession, and with parents who are still struggling to make ends meet. Ask them if they aspire to follow their parents' example, and most will answer with a resounding "No."

Ask young people if they dream of spending eight hours a day in a four-by-four cubicle, conforming to a schedule someone else will determine, and most will answer: "Not a chance!"

Middle-class Americans have not yet benefited from the economic recovery. According to the Census Bureau, the income of the median American household has not shown a statistically significant increase since 2009, while living costs have steadily increased.

The shrinking job market is a global problem. Plummeting gas prices are impacting jobs in Canada and market forces are decimating jobs in Australia. The slowdown in China's economy has dramatically reduced its demand for imported goods and services, leading to job losses in countries that manufacture and supply them.

My view is that it makes no sense to relinquish control of your income to a third party. When you have no control over your income, your choices diminish. When you control your income, your choices increase. Network marketing will always have the welcome mat out for those who refuse to let others dictate their paycheck.

If you keep your antenna up, you'll come across people with a range of reasons to start a network marketing business. Some will be seeking to fund a better lifestyle now, while others will want to take the pressure off their financial situation by reducing their debts. A few will be seeking to safeguard their future by paying off their mortgage or boosting their financial portfolio. Network marketing has opportunities for all of them.

The technological advances that have eaten into the traditional workforce have been a boon to network marketers.

- Your online store and back office will be as sophisticated as those of any large business.

- You won't be curbed by unnecessary restrictions. As long as you operate within the laws and guidelines that protect your customers and other network marketers, you are free to work when and how you want.

- You won't be floundering about on your own. You'll receive ongoing training and support from your sponsor and your corporation. For the most part, your network marketing education will be accessible online and free.

- You will find a wealth of support from industry professionals who have built successful businesses and are willing to show you how. What differentiates network marketing from a costly college or university education is that you can earn as you learn.

- You won't be confined to a territory. You can start your business with your existing contacts, or you can generate contacts through referrals, trade shows, markets, or social media. Many companies have seamless global plans that enable you to build your business worldwide. Your next international flight could be a tax-deductible business trip.

- Most network companies offer the opportunity to earn expenses-paid incentive trips every year and stage annual conferences in exciting destinations such as Las Vegas, Orlando, and Maui.

As a network marketing leader you won't be creating a demand; you'll be meeting a demand. People are flocking to network marketing. Over a hundred thousand people worldwide sign a direct sales agreement every day, and twenty-five thousand of those agreements are signed in America. Your mission will be that more of them sign with you.

As part of my research for this book I spearheaded the launch of an American network marketing company into Australia. The launch was a spectacular success with more than three thousand independent contractors enrolling in the first ten months and first year sales touching $10 million.

Even more significantly, I worked from my home on the central coast of California, seven thousand miles away. I traveled to Australia a few times, but as many successful network marketers do, I lived where I wanted to live and I worked where I wanted to work. The opportunity to build a business in any geographic location without having to uproot your family or leave your friends behind makes network marketing especially appealing.

Achieving financial freedom by helping others achieve financial freedom is a concept as simple as it is genius. But here's a word of caution. As many aspiring network marketers have discovered, there's a vast difference between being an entrepreneur and a *wantrepreneur*. Almost everyone wants it. Only a few are willing to work for it.

Answer these questions to reveal if you're equipped to lead your own network marketing empire:

- ❑ Do I want financial freedom?
- ❑ Am I willing to conquer my fears?
- ❑ Am I willing to eliminate my excuses?
- ❑ Am I willing to take risks?
- ❑ Am I willing to work?
- ❑ Am I willing to learn?
- ❑ Am I willing to block out the doubters and detractors?
- ❑ Am I willing to accept that if it's not working for me, it's because I'm not doing enough, or I'm doing the wrong things?
- ❑ Am I willing to change instead of expecting others to change?
- ❑ Am I ready to start now?

If you checked all the boxes you have demonstrated that you have a positive attitude and a willingness to take consistent action, and that you're open to having a flexible approach.

It's time to transfer your dreams from your *wish* list to your *do* list, and make them come true.

CHAPTER 2

The First Steps to Building Your Empire

Our family enjoys spending time together at theme parks. As we always have a number of restless little ones in our party, we stay at park-owned hotels that offer early entry into the park. With an hour's head start on the crowds, we can enjoy the most popular attractions without waiting in long lines.

On our last family vacation, the *Cars* attraction at Disneyland was a big hit. There were no lines when we arrived, and we managed several spins around the track before I decided to wait while my family took one last spin. As I was waiting, a tsunami of people swarmed toward me. The park had opened for general entry, and it seemed that everyone was heading for the *Cars* ride. Within minutes, the wait time on the electronic board clicked from "no waiting" to more than two hours. Timing is everything!

Compare starting a network marketing business today with gaining early entry to the park. According to the WFDSA, the number of people starting a network marketing business has hit all-time highs for the last two consecutive years, and the wave shows no sign of abating. The sooner you start building your business the more likely you are to catch the new wave of growth.

Research commissioned by the leading industry magazine, *Direct Selling News*, shows where customers purchased a direct sales product in the previous six months:

- Online: 66 percent
- Craft show or farmers' market: 64 percent
- Group setting: 55 percent
- One-on-one consultation: 47 percent
- Demonstration: 44 percent
- Seminar or presentation: 24 percent

The business has not reached close to its potential. Out of America's 320,000,000 people, there are currently only 16,000,000 independent contractors operating a direct selling business.

Out of the 600,000,000 combined populations of South and Central America, there are only 14,000,000 independent contractors.

Across all the Western European countries, there are only an estimated 13,000,000 independent contractors.

Australia's population of 23,000,000 has approximately half a million independent contractors.

Although statistics can't be verified in the Asia Pacific and Eastern European regions, indications are that network marketing is experiencing explosive growth due to an increase in lifestyle expectations.

Given the sorry state of the traditional job market, all of the above spells O-P-P-O-R-T-U-N-I-T-Y.

As every entrepreneur knows, one of the keys to opportunity is identifying a trend before everyone else does. The sooner you start your network marketing business, the greater the opportunity you'll have to ride the front of the next wave of growth.

Latest statistics from the American Direct Selling Association (DSA) indicate that 70 percent of direct sellers sell person-to-person (including door-to-door), 23 percent sell through parties and group presentations (including online and face-to-face), and 7 percent by other methods.

While sales are the foundation of a network marketing business, few people achieve financial freedom by going it alone. The way to earn the highest incomes is to attract good people and mentor them to their highest potential. True leaders know that the key to success is to build a winning team around you, and that is the crux of a network marketing business. *You lead to succeed.*

This book contains valuable lessons for any team, corporate, or organizational leader. Anyone can manage employees who can't afford to leave. But that skims close to exploitation. The test of a leader is how you lead those who are with you by choice.

Demotivated, disinterested, or disgruntled staff cost the owners of small and large businesses billions of dollars a year. We have all been on the receiving end of indifferent service, in store or at the end of a phone. We've all met with a frosty reception when showing up for an appointment. Most of us have switched service providers, walked out of a store without buying, or taken our business elsewhere as a result.

When I was writing this book I entered a store to buy an item I purchase often. The store was almost empty, and the staff was congregating in one area. I could not find what I was looking for and walked over to ask for help. One staff member reluctantly followed me back to the area I had been fruitlessly searching. When I asked her to check if there was more inventory at the back of the store she said, "We don't carry much stock here. There's a better selection on the Internet." Before I had reached the exit she was back chatting with the other staff members.

A retailer that understands the power of community is Apple. Walk into any Apple store and you instantly feel the vibe. That's why Apple is the world's most successful retailer when measured by sales per square foot of store space. It has successfully built a community of proud staff and loyal customers. But Apple is the exception, not the norm.

....

Before you start building your organization, prepare yourself to lead others by taking these five personal leadership steps.

STEP ONE: YOU CAN'T EXPECT TO INSPIRE OTHERS UNLESS YOU ARE INSPIRED

Write your own *I have a dream* script and commit to making it a reality. A powerful personal goal will overshadow your doubts, distractions, disappointments, and detractors. A timid goal is hardly worth setting. It takes an exciting goal to get you back on your feet after you stumble, or back on track when you lose your way.

If you don't have a goal that makes your heart leap, fast-forward a few years and picture your life:

- What is your annual income?
- Where do you live?
- Is your home mortgage-free?
- Where will your next vacation be?
- What car do you drive?
- What college or university do your kids attend?
- What are you doing in your leisure time?
- Who are the people who surround you?
- How do you contribute to your community?

- What does your financial portfolio look like?
- What charities do you support?
- What makes you happy?

When you have defined your vision of success, zoom back to the present. What will you accomplish in your first year?

One year is the ideal time frame for á first goal. It's close enough that you'll feel it, yet gives you enough time to achieve it. Annual goals become milestones toward our ultimate financial and lifestyle destination.

> If your goal doesn't scare you a little,
> it's not big enough.

STEP TWO: COMMIT TO SUCCEEDING BY ELIMINATING YOUR EXCUSES

Zeroing in on what's wrong in your life instead of what's right is self-indulgent and a little narcissistic. No one is going to give you a free pass because you've taken a few hits in your life.

I could blame my alcoholic dad when I feel anxious. I could just as easily credit my pioneering forebears for my courage. I could remind myself that my grandfather sacrificed his life for our freedom, or that my mother never gave up and never gave in no matter how many knocks she took.

You are not a product of one experience in your life. You are a product of every experience. Sometimes it takes a wider lens to gain perspective and find the strength to move on from past fears and failures.

We make our own choices in life and if you're seeking financial freedom, you have to know you can't make excuses and money at the same time.

Seven sins guaranteed to sabotage your success:

1. Undervaluing the opportunity: Don't underestimate the potential of your business because it cost you so little to start it.

2. Overestimating the challenge: Start with the strengths you have and develop the strengths you need.

3. Overvaluing other people's opinions: Other people's opinions don't pay your bills.

4. Underestimating yourself: You have a greater power inside you than any challenge facing you.

5. Overrelying on others: We don't all get an experienced sponsor or supportive family.

6. Overcomplicating your strategy: If you try to do everything, you risk accomplishing nothing.

7. Underperforming the hours: You won't get results from work you don't do.

What makes this business powerful is that we don't have to carry our mistakes or missteps with us. Every day is a fresh start. Whatever brought you to this point in your business, or whatever mistakes you make along the way, you won't drive your business forward by fixating on the rearview mirror. The only antidote to anxiety is action.

Press the reset button and focus on making the right moves for your business each day. Not enough sales? Find more customers! Not enough team members? Sponsor more people! Not enough team members are performing? Become a better leader!

As long as you give yourself a 10 out of 10 for commitment you can learn the skills. Commit to your business and build it one day, one step at a time. Without commitment your dream is a hallucination.

STEP THREE: BECOME AN AVID
COLLECTOR OF REWARDS

The more experiences you gather on your journey, the more exciting and rewarding it will be. You can compare building your network marketing empire to taking a road trip. The journey is what makes it exciting.

Don't become so entranced with your destination that you forget to seek out and enjoy every experience along the way. Turn your company compensation plan into your roadmap. It has all your milestones and rewards clearly mapped out. Aim to achieve all of them. Never bypass an experience, nor let a reward go unclaimed.

If you are unclear about the rewards available to you, ask your sponsor or distributor services representative to run through the plan with you. Make sure you know the answers to these questions:

- What are my deadlines for achieving the new distributor rewards?
- What sales will give me the maximum sales bonus each month?
- How will I be recognized for achieving key milestones?
- What bonuses will I receive for sponsoring others?
- Will the bonuses increase if I sponsor multiple people in a single month?
- What bonuses will I earn for promoting up the ranks?
- What will I earn when my team members promote?
- Is there a company incentive trip I can achieve each year?
- What are the qualifying dates to achieve it?
- When and where is the annual Convention?
- What annual awards can I aim for?

- Does our company offer monthly incentives?

It's the rewards and experiences we gather en route that fuel our belief in the business and inspire us to keep moving forward.

I was speaking for an insurance company that paid an instant $500 bonus to its associates each time they referred someone who signed up. When I held up five $100 bills and asked an associate sitting in the front row, "If I gave you this money right now, what would you spend it on?" he answered, without a second's hesitation, "New sunglasses!" I could feel the passion ten feet away.

A few days later I made a similar offer to an audience of jewelry consultants. This time the answer shot at me from several directions: "Shoes!" Again the passion was palpable.

Rewards come in all sizes, and they can all pack a powerful punch. When you understand that instant gratification is a powerful motivator you will become a better leader.

> Happiness doesn't come from big pieces of great success, but from small, daily achievements.
>
> BENJAMIN FRANKLIN

STEP FOUR: ASK FOR SUPPORT

When your family and friends understand how important your business is to you they're more likely to support you. They'll be more enthusiastic if you involve them in your goal:

"I want the two of us to take a fabulous vacation without stressing about the cost."

"If I can eliminate our credit card debts, we will save more than $3,000 a year in interest payments."

"If we upgrade our car to a Range Rover we can take more family trips."

STEP FIVE: GET TO WORK

You don't get paid for believing in your dreams. The more hours you work, the more progress you will make. As long as you keep your goal in your sights and stay in your lane you will succeed. Don't allow disappointment or distractions to tempt you to leave the path. No matter how bumpy it gets, keep moving forward.

Inevitably there will be times when your business will feel like an obstacle course. That's when you need to revisit your goal to get the boost you need to tackle those obstacles head-on.

> If you're not overcoming an obstacle, change how you're tackling it! A leader doesn't expect others to change or the situation to change. A leader thinks: *I must change!*

When you know exactly where you're going, and you're committed to the journey, you will be ready to invite others to join you. It's time to show you how to build your empire.

••

The Importance of Staying Focused
Scott and Cindy Monroe, founders, Thirty-One Gifts, LLC

We humans have a tough time staying focused. We blame it on television, the Internet, loud music, or too much high fructose corn syrup, among a myriad of excuses, but a lack of focus comes at a high cost to our businesses and our lives. It can lead to fatigue, confusion, and weariness. It can lead to us failing those we lead.

With all the noise that surrounds us it's easy for our vision to become blurred. But we have to find focus amid the chaos of our world to move forward in a purposeful manner.

Have you noticed that the majority of truly exceptional photographs focus on a single person or object? Whereas amateur photographers may try to get everything in the photo in focus, experienced photographers use a "narrow depth of field" to focus on the beauty of one subject.

The same is true about life. We must find ways to narrow our personal "depth of field" and discover the beauty of focusing on one subject.

Many things in life challenge our ability to focus. We may focus on too much at one time, focus too long on one thing, or focus on the wrong things and lose our direction.

Step back and evaluate how focused you are on your business:

- *Daily tasks.* Do you struggle to decide what you need to tackle first?

- *Business conversations.* Are you "that person" who tries to sell, book, recruit in one short conversation in the grocery store?

- *Product displays.* Are you displaying too many products? Are you exhausted by how much packing up you have to do at the end of your presentations?

- *Product demonstrations.* Are you confusing your customers by offering them too many choices?

- *Social media.* Are you oversharing? We're going to be brutally honest here. No one likes people who post too much, or who send out random requests to join the latest game craze.

- *Team training events.* Do you focus on what your group needs most, or on everything?

- *Time with your children.* Have you noticed that they always behave better when their siblings aren't around? Are you giving each of them quality one-on-one time?

- *Time with your spouse.* Are you letting television, your phone, a juicy novel, or even your kids keep you from those personal interactions you had when you first fell in love?

Even good things can easily become distractions, and as a couple working together in the business we've had to learn the hard way that it doesn't take much for distraction to become destruction.

● ● ●

We've implemented these simple guidelines to help us stay focused at work and at home with our family:

- *Set clear goals.* You can't get anywhere efficiently if you don't know where you're going.

- *Communicate, communicate, communicate.* Let your family and friends know where you want to focus and let them hold you accountable. Open and frequent communication helps us find balance as partners at home with our family, at work with our staff, and with all the independent consultants who rely on us.

- *Do one thing well instead of many mediocre things.* The old adage "Jack of all trades, master of none" is even more relevant when we have so many choices in life. None of us is omniscient or omnipresent. Let's leave that to the man upstairs. You will never be good at everything, so be great at a few things.

- *Work smart.* Work to your strengths. By focusing solely on our strengths, a multitude of distractions automatically falls off our plate. Seek out people with strengths that complement yours, so that you can focus on the things you do well. When we started our business we learned that one party would pay for someone to clean the house. Although both took a similar amount of time, parties were more a productive use of our time.

- *Budget your resources.* Money, time, emotions, face-to-face interactions, and sleep are all important. If you go into debt with any one of them it won't turn out well.

- *Stop comparing yourself with others.* You can't stay focused if you're always worrying about what other people are doing, getting, or achieving. Obsessing about other people's lives or businesses can eat away at your time and emotions. And it won't improve your life. We can get so stressed about how another person is sponsoring or breaking the rules by "selling on Facebook" that we forget to make a positive impact on our own circle.

- *Pick things that will "move the needle."* Invest your time and energy wisely and don't waste your resources on things you can't do anything about, or that won't move you forward.

- *Spend wisely.* We believe that people get into network marketing to make money, not spend money. Make good decisions about how much product and materials you need to support your business.

- *Invest in the right people.* Learn to deal with those "super-needy" folks in your organization. Keep encouraging them, but don't spend your time trying to make it happen for them. If you're succeeding in this business, you have a whole team to take care of, and you can't afford to let one person monopolize your time and energy.

Life is a gift. It's too short to spend agonizing over things that don't matter. Find a clear sense of direction and work hard to minimize your distractions. Zoom in a little closer, focus that lens, and do what you need to do to make your business a truly fulfilling experience for yourself, your family, and your community.

PART TWO

Grow Your Network

CHAPTER 3

Developing
a Community

Network marketing is an emotionally charged business. We're drawn to it because we're passionate about our goals. But our journey toward achieving them is often a turbulent one. One minute we can be full speed ahead and the next we're hitting unexpected roadblocks.

That's why network marketers need the support of a leader who understands the unpredictable nature of the business. A leader committed to supporting, encouraging, and guiding us, through good times and bad.

Network marketing leaders never underestimate the influence they can have over other people's lives. Their greatest satisfaction comes from inspiring others to pursue their dreams, and mentoring them on their journey to success.

If you center your business on your products, it will always be vulnerable to every new, improved, or different product that comes along. If you center your business on money, there will always be new income opportunities to entice your team members away.

When you focus your business on people, they will feel stronger, stay longer, and perform better. Build your business as a community that will attract good people and encourage them to stay.

Our need to belong to a community is powerful. We're happiest when we have a loving family, a network of good friends, a supportive workplace. When you build your network marketing business as a community you will draw people in, keep them engaged, and inspire them to grow.

People will join you for many reasons. They'll join because they are passionate about your company's products or services. They'll join because they're attracted to the income-producing opportunities. Some will carefully consider their decision to join and others will act impulsively. Every team member will bring different talents, circumstances, experiences, and expectations to your organization.

Whatever their motivation, it will be their experiences *after* they join that will determine what they do with the opportunity you have given them. The more rewarding their experiences, the more reluctant they will be to leave—even when they hit slow or rough patches in their businesses. We go where we are invited but we stay where we feel inspired, involved, and appreciated.

Create a community that will fulfill the social, emotional, and financial needs of its members. A community where they will be eager to work, encouraged to learn, and excited to grow. When they're actively engaged, fewer will underperform or drift away. They'll work through their challenges and setbacks instead of giving up on the business or moving on to something new when things don't go according to plan.

You can build your network marketing community locally, across many states, or on other continents. A community is not defined by geography but by the emotional connection we have with those who share our vision and values.

Few corporations appreciate the value of creating an inclusive environment for their employees. Their structure makes it impossible to provide everyone an equal opportunity to pursue leadership positions in the company. The closer you get to the top, the fewer opportunities there will be to advance. Most likely you'll have to compete against coworkers to reach the C-suite. It's not a recipe for a healthy community where cooperation, consideration, and collaboration are key.

Successful network marketing leaders take pride in creating a supportive community where everyone has an equal opportunity to grow. A community that offers unlimited opportunities for the most ambitious members to advance, but where everyone will be valued, regardless of the size of their contribution.

Design your business as a community that every team member will be proud to belong to, where members are inspired to grow and encouraged to support each other. When they feel bonded by a common vision, they will be happy to offer mutual support and encouragement.

....

One of the questions leaders often share with me is: *I spend a lot of my time supporting my team members, but where can I get support? I'm not supposed to share any negatives with my team members, or post them on our leader pages, so how can I find help with my problems?*

That's when the power of belonging to like-minded communities beyond your own becomes apparent. There are many leadership and networking groups around, but no one faces the same challenges as much as leaders within your own company. If you can't find a support group, create one!

I asked Renée Hornbaker, the chief financial officer of Stream Energy, a network marketing opportunity that grew to become one of the top fifteen direct sales companies in the world in less than ten years, to share an initiative her company implemented.

"As our sales force was predominantly male, we decided to sponsor a three-day 'Women of Power' retreat to specifically support our female leaders," said Renée.

One of the initiatives the leaders themselves implemented from the retreat was deciding to support each other. Realizing that they shared common challenges, they formed accountability groups outside their own teams to support and hold each other accountable for their goals.

While they were reluctant to share their limitations within their teams, they felt able to openly discuss their challenges with each other. They also saw the accountability groups as a way to pool their skills and experiences to better support their people.

These support groups were so strong they soon extended beyond webinar meet-ups to leaders flying to meet each other. "A grassroots effort started by some of our top leaders helped foster the spirit of community that we are eager to encourage company-wide," said Renée. "We're now looking at how we can support other communities within our organization such as Hispanics and millennials."

It's easy to abandon a network marketing business. Your team members have risked nothing to start it and they will lose nothing if they move on. The only way to stop them leaving is to create an experience that is more rewarding than just the financial gains.

When team members feel socially and emotionally engaged, they won't be tempted to jump ship on a whim. They'll pause and weigh the true cost of leaving. Few people walk away from a group that has become significant in their lives.

The concept is simple: Make it easy for people to join you and hard for them to leave.

Network marketing leaders never overvalue the contribution they can make to the success of their businesses, nor undervalue the contribution others make. They use their influence to build their team members' belief and confidence in their products, the business, and themselves. Leaders want their voice saying, "You can do this!" to be heard louder than their team members' inner voices saying, "This is too hard."

You won't be able to influence every team member. Each person will bring different aspirations, talents, circumstances, and experiences to the team. How much time and effort they apply to their business will be determined by how much they want it, and how willing they are to work for it. Even the most skilled leader can't bring out something that doesn't exist inside of someone. But you'll be able to influence many. On some you'll have an impact beyond your wildest imagination.

Envision the community you would want to belong to. I'm sure that it would be a community where you feel welcome and included, where you'll find friendship and support, where you'll be inspired and empowered to grow. When your vision is clear, start creating that community.

Now, picture the kind of leader you would want to have. Most likely it will be a leader who believes in you, inspires you to aim high, and helps you reach your goals. A leader who takes an interest in you beyond the financial contribution you make. When your vision is clear, work on becoming that leader.

CHAPTER 4

Create an Upbeat, Can-Do Culture

Winning communities are built by design, not default, by leaders who have a clear vision and strong values. The magic is in the detail. Take a proactive approach to turning your vision into an inspiring, energizing experience for every team member. Figure 4-1 shows how you must incorporate many elements to create a successful network marketing community.

Figure 4-1 The Dynamics of a Winning Community

In the following chapters I will show you how to blend all the elements into your business. I'll start with the most important: *Culture*.

Think of culture as the personality of your community. Everyone performs better in an inspiring environment surrounded by positive, like-minded people. Plan on creating a vibrant community with an upbeat, optimistic, can-do culture.

Make your presence felt at every opportunity by communicating your vision clearly and consistently. Never let an opportunity pass to fuel your team members' hope, excitement, and belief. The more often you express your vision, the more ingrained into your culture it will become.

Don't ever be tempted to share your stresses with your team members. It's never professional and always a downer. Be a bright light in their lives. Projecting an aura of calm and happiness is as important as projecting an aura of success.

The most powerful word in any community is *we*. Network marketers are almost always free spirits. We don't respond to rules and regulations. We want collaboration and inclusion. Younger team members expect it.

Every time you use the *we* word, you share ownership of your culture, as compared to imposing your vision and values on your team members. A sure sign that you have created an inclusive community will be hearing your team members using *we* when discussing their businesses.

Culture will have a stronger influence over your business than just the "feel-good" factor. It will be how you drive performance and lift results.

Every network marketing compensation plan is designed to reward the behaviors that lead to growth. When you match your performance expectations to the plan, you're helping your team members reap the maximum rewards from their businesses. The more money they make, the more positive they will feel.

Incorporate these results-generating action statements into your culture:

- We place an order every month to stay active.
- We're always our own best customer.
- We aim for the highest commission level each month.
- We don't wait until the end of the month to place orders.
- We offer the business to everyone.
- We aim to achieve every incentive.
- We attend all team meetings.
- We go to Convention.
- We do trade shows, farmers' markets, or vendor events to revitalize our contacts.

There's no greater compliment you can pay a team member than to set high expectations. It's the ultimate demonstration of your belief in him or her.

Not every team member is going to want, or be in a position, to meet your high expectations. But you don't need everyone on board. If you inspire the majority to lift their game your business will benefit. Many top leaders will tell you: "When I first started my business I simply did what my sponsor told me to do."

The clearer your culture, the less likely that it will be hijacked by the weaker personalities in your team. A few guidelines will ensure a level playing field for all team members as they pursue their individual goals:

1. We respect each other.
2. We support each other.
3. We appreciate everyone's contribution.
4. We're always professional.

5. We operate in a spirit of fun and friendship.

6. We keep it positive.

7. We're a gossip-free zone.

8. We deal with our disagreements in private.

Above all, don't let the voice of jaded or negative team members speak louder than yours. The morale of your entire community depends on it.

Consider the impact your culture will have on new team members. What first impressions do you want them to have? If the atmosphere is flat, or they sense tension or dissension in the ranks, they may doubt their decision to join. A vibrant culture will validate their decision, and they'll feel energized and excited from the start.

If your business has lost its fire, the only way to fix it is to find new team members. You won't change attitudes overnight and there is no better way to energize demotivated team members than an influx of new people. Their excitement and enthusiasm will lift the spirits of other team members, or help them move on. It's almost impossible to restore power to a network marketing business without new people.

Everyone who joins your team will entrust his or her dreams to you. They need to feel confident they can trust you to lead them all the way to achieving these dreams. No one wants an indecisive leader. We want confidence, certainty, and, above all, clarity.

By clearly and consistently communicating your culture you will become a more influential leader.

· ·

Build a Business with a Soul
Bob Hipple, CEO, Damsel in Defense

When my son was an F-16 pilot in the U.S. Air Force, his job was to train pilots entering one of the most elite teams in the entire world. While visiting his base I saw a mural on a building that had one large word written across it: *BLAZE*. Under it were these words: *Building Leaders, Advancing Integrity, Service Before Self, and Excellence in All We Do.*

The Air Force training program is designed to take goal-oriented, driven individuals and turn them into world-class pilots who have honor, teamwork, and service as their core values.

The same values embody the essence of building a successful network marketing business. Your job is to take goal-oriented, driven individuals and turn them into service-oriented leaders.

You are not in the sales business. You're in the people business, and you'll grow by finding and developing people who are not just talented sellers and recruiters, but also people who can work as a team to promote more leaders who share integrity, service, and a passion for excellence as their core values.

Building a business with a soul is more than making as much money as you can, or seeing the people in your organization as cogs in a wheel that churns out more money. It's making a difference in the lives of the people in your organization. When you do this you will make all the money you want.

Great leaders know that their success is closely tied to the success of the people in their organization. When they succeed, you succeed.

We rarely remember people because they made a lot of money. We remember them for what they added to society. Your network marketing business is an opportunity to make a positive impact on the lives of thousands of people by building a business with a soul. Too many people think that if you have a great product then you will have a great business. It helps, but think back to the last time you went to a restaurant for dinner. If the food was good but the service was horrible, you thought, "I will never come here again."

Your most important product is the opportunity for people to achieve their dreams. Give them a place they can belong, and never miss an opportunity to help them grow. Anyone can copy a product and a compensation plan. But when you get your culture right it is very, very hard to copy.

Outstanding businesses are built on people, not profit. If profit is your only focus then every decision you make will be about money. When this attitude bleeds through to your organization it will negatively affect your growth. Focus on people first. Profits will come.

The greatest power in any business is "People Power." No matter how good your products are and no matter how much potential your company seems to have, what will determine the success or failure of your business will always be the effort, dedication, and success of the people on your team.

CHAPTER 5

Engage Your Team Members on Facebook

Nowhere will the culture of your community be more visible than on your group Facebook page. Facebook is the face of your community and where the majority of your team members will engage with you and each other. Make sure your page reflects the vibrant culture of your community, and the message that greets every visitor is an inspiring and energizing, "Welcome to our winning team!"

Too often I am invited to join a group only to be welcomed with a stern notice outlining "Rules for This Page" or "Posts must be approved by an Admin." It chills my ardor instantly, as it suggests the leaders have lost control of their community.

I feel the same when I see leaders posting plaintive requests for feedback. If your team members are not responding, take it as a sign that they're not engaging. That's when you have to remind yourself that you cannot expect people to change. You must change.

Update your cover photo often. Even the most inspiring image will lose its luster over time. Keep your page fresh with images of new products, the next incentive destination, or the host city for your annual Convention.

Liberally sprinkle positive, inspiring affirmations throughout your group:

- *We never lose. We win or improve!*
- *Your business won't build itself. If you want it, work for it!*
- *The only antidote to anxiety is action!*
- *The biggest mistake you can make is being afraid to make one!*
- *Defeat is a temporary condition. Giving up makes it permanent!*
- *Don't get upset at the results you didn't get from the work you didn't do!*
- *If you want it you'll find a way; if you don't you'll find an excuse!*
- *If it's worth having it's worth working for!*

Seemingly nonsensical quotes that carry a grain of truth inside them are also a smart way to make key points:

- *I was going to change the world today, but then something sparkly caught my eye!*
- *If at first you do succeed, try not to look astonished!*

••

For more positive and lively affirmations, connect with Mary Christensen on Facebook at this web address: http://www.facebook.com/pages/Mary-Christensen/211167465605116?sk=wall.

••

Make it a team effort. Encouraging all team members to share their favorite affirmations and quotes will reinforce that you are a winning team, not a *whining* team. Frequently highlight the successes of individual team members and encourage them to share a business tip every time you do.

Create and upload short videos to your page, or post videos you have permission to share. The same person saying the same stuff over and over can be a hard sell.

Give all team members their time in the spotlight by sharing their stories. Profiling your smaller performers shows that you value all team members, not just your top performers. Make a big deal of it when team members promote to new status levels.

Keep it businesslike. Don't let your group page be dominated by drawn-out personal stories or issues that have nothing to do with growing a business.

My response when I am tagged with a request for a donation to a charity or cause is to hit the delete key. It's not because I don't care; it's because it's the wrong platform. When you decline to support personal agendas on your page you are not rejecting the cause. You're rejecting the inappropriate methods being employed.

Don't be afraid to take a tough approach to protecting your culture. Team morale is at stake. Remove posts that are long-winded or self-indulgent. Just because a person is having a bad day doesn't give that person permission to bring everyone else down too. And the only response to posts such as, "I'm thinking of quitting and have some inventory I want to sell" is to remove the person!

· ·

Keys to Creating a Winning Culture!
Tom and Kelly Gaines, Founders, Pink Zebra Home

Network marketing has always been an opportunity bursting with potential. To achieve your highest potential, you'll need a whole community of people who believe in the same things as you, and will work with you to create a winning culture.

As we built our business we quickly discovered three keys that are necessary to creating a winning culture.

1. Your Actions Become Your Culture

Set high standards for how you will treat each other and match your actions to your beliefs. Leaders seek to serve their teams and are always willing to go the extra mile to make their experience the best possible.

When we started our company we could not afford to stage a conference. But we knew our people needed one, so we rented a twenty-six-foot truck, loaded it to capacity, and with our entire staff and family on board drove it twenty-two hours from our office in Texas to our Convention site in Florida. Then we did the entire setup ourselves to create a magical experience for all. Your culture will be based on what you do, not what you say!

2. Remove People Who Don't Fit Your Culture

If you have people who threaten your culture you must remove them. It's not enough to set clear standards; you must be willing to enforce them. Be willing to privately discuss infractions with offenders, but ultimately you must take action. Talk to problem people immediately but never do it in public.

When people abuse your social media forum by complaining, or attacking others, you should not hesitate to remove them. When your standards are transparent and unyielding, your people will rally around you. You will know you've been successful when you see your people protecting your culture as vigorously as you do.

3. Meetings Are Oxygen to Your Culture

When I was younger, I started a catering company that supplied food and drinks for high-end apartment social events.

Curious as to why the owners spent this kind of money on their residents, I asked one manager what value she gained from the events. She said, "If they meet a friend they will renew their lease on their apartment."

We have mirrored that approach in our business. We travel to different meetings across the country to provide a place for people to connect and learn. Thousands of people who know each other only on Facebook can meet in person and strengthen friendships that began online.

Your number one challenge as a leader will be keeping people involved. You may not be able to match the scale of a corporate event but you can provide what really matters, and that's a place to build and strengthen relationships.

CHAPTER 6

Healthy Relationships = Healthy Business

A healthy culture will influence how your team members interact in all their business relationships, with their corporate partner, their customers, and their competitors.

CULTURE AND CORPORATE

A mutually respectful relationship between distributors and their corporate partner is critical to the success of any network marketing business. You are in this business together, and you must fiercely protect the partnership. Never allow a "them and us" attitude to develop.

Healthy relationships lead to healthy businesses. Don't leave this aspect of your business to chance. Constantly and consistently reinforce the value of the partnership between team members and the company by stressing that:

- We read all company communications.
- We participate in company training.

- We take advantage of company tools and resources.
- We embrace company initiatives.
- We attend company events.
- We adhere to company policies.
- We're all in this together.

Make company-provided incentives and events the core of your business. Promote them vigorously throughout your organization. Expertly leveraged, they are an incredibly cost-effective way to drive your business.

You won't always agree with everything your corporate partner does. It will sometimes make mistakes or implement unwelcome changes. You can almost count on management changes (take them as a reminder of why you're in business for yourself!). Company chiefs are expected to make tough decisions to keep up with innovations and evolutions in the market. That's their job!

When team members support the company 100 percent they won't be distracted by decisions they cannot control, or drawn into discussions that won't make the slightest difference. Consistently communicate the message, "The company always has our best interests at heart," and your team members will learn to accept that no company gets it right every time, or can please every distributor all the time.

CULTURE AND CUSTOMERS

Taking care of customers is our business, and the clearer your guidelines are in this area, the more likely it is that community members will do so.

This is another example of the power of liberally using the inclusive *we* word. Established guidelines will take the guesswork out of how to take care of customers. For example:

- We let them know that we appreciate them.
- We go the extra mile to make them happy.
- We make a follow-up call after every sale.
- We keep in touch regularly.
- We don't pressure them.
- We keep them engaged and interested with regular news, tips, and teasers.
- We offer them all the business opportunity.

. . . .

More customers will be lost to indifference than be lured away by competitors. If you're not taking care of your customers they'll find someone who will.

. . . .

CULTURE AND COMPETITORS

One of the achievements our industry is most proud of is the spirit of cooperation and consideration in which we operate. Direct selling companies even worked together to establish self-regulatory codes of conduct that go far beyond government regulations. One of your responsibilities as a leader is to carry that torch for the good of the whole industry. How you represent your industry and relate to your competitors is a measure of your authenticity and integrity.

You will not be with your team members all the time. You must rely on them to carry your culture into their communities. That's why your messaging must be crystal clear:

- We buy from other network marketers wherever possible.
- We never disparage our competitors.
- We don't offer the business to distributors who are active in other companies.

Your team members will support your strict guidelines if they understand the reason behind them and can personally relate to them. I use these messages to reinforce my "we're in this together" belief:

- *When you disparage competitors, you make yourself look bad.*

- *When you criticize a competitor, you're hurting someone who is trying to build his or her business the same as you are trying to build yours.*

- *When you compare our products to other products, you draw attention to your competitors.*

- *When you knock competing products, people will think that you're feeling threatened by them.*

The "our products are the best" message is well past its use-by date. Customers want specifics about how your products will make them feel better, look better. They want to know how your services will make their lives easier, or save them money. If they're interested in comparing products and services, they'll do their own research.

CULTURE AND CONFLICT

In any community that encompasses a range of personalities, the occasional conflict is inevitable. These ten tips will help you deal with delicate situations . . . while keeping your sanity intact!

1. Take Ownership of the Solution

This is your business. Even if you didn't create the problem you will most likely need to be involved in the resolution. Drama within the ranks can be a tantalizing distraction, and the longer conflicts drag on, the more havoc they can wreak on the morale of all team members. The sooner you find a solution, the sooner everyone can get back to work.

2. Listen Without Judging
You'll often find that people aren't seeking advice or approval. They simply want a chance to share their side of the story.

3. Don't Take Sides
Try to involve all parties in finding a solution. Ask each party: "I need your help resolving this. How would you suggest we move forward?"

4. Be Willing to Compromise
Very few issues are black and white. Think of yourself as a moderator and help both parties find a compromise.

5. Avoid Confrontation
If you start feeling emotionally involved, or you're tempted to react impulsively, take a few breaths. Go for a walk. Sleep on it. Do whatever it takes to recover your composure before you take the next step.

6. Don't Be Drawn into Lengthy, "She Said/I Said" Exchanges
The first person to stop always wins.

7. Don't Make It Personal and Don't Take It Personally
Most of us have said things in the heat of the moment that we've regretted afterward.

8. Sometimes the Best Course of Action Is to Do Nothing
I learned this one from experience. Flash-in-the-pan conflicts may sort themselves out faster without your interference. Don't ignore them but don't fan the flames if you feel the flare-up is losing its heat.

9. Forgive

By harboring resentments you give the other person control of your emotions. You have to forgive before you can move on.

10. Be Proactive

The stronger your culture, the fewer the conflicts that will arise. Reinforce your culture by communicating it frequently and enforcing it when necessary.

"We're a business family. We support each other as any family would do."

"We don't take disagreements personally and we don't make them personal."

"We accept and respect each other."

Anyone can lead when things are going well. It's how you respond to crises and challenges that will mark you as a true leader. Above all, maintain your perspective. There's a crazy person on every team, and if not, it's probably you!

• • •

As your organization grows, a clearly defined culture will be critical to your success. When you have only a handful of team members you can deal with most situations as they arise. When you have hundreds of team members you can guarantee that your organization will include a wide range of personalities, perspectives, and circumstances. If you don't have a clearly defined and executed culture you could easily lose control.

Create and nurture a vibrant culture in your business and your team members will be excited to participate, eager to contribute, and empowered to grow!

CHAPTER 7

Walking the Talk

There are no management positions in network marketing, only sales and leadership ones. You need to master both.

The Holy Grail of network marketing is duplication, and the only credible way to lead your organization is to walk the talk. The example you set as a role model will directly influence how your people perform. As goes the leader, so goes the team.

Lead your team by becoming a champion for your business. Champions are role models. They show by example that the way to build a six-figure-income business is to purposefully and consistently perform the core tasks.

Spend as much time as possible at the front line of your business, and always on the ten most productive activities.

Personal activity:

- Working your contacts
- Making new contacts
- Scheduling appointments
- Marketing your products
- Servicing your customers

- Prospecting for team members
- Sponsoring new team members

Team activity:

- Supporting new recruits
- Coaching all team members
- Mentoring potential leaders

This list is not multiple choice. You have to perform all the activities. If there are gaps in your business, for example, you do not have enough team members, you must prioritize the tasks that will close the gap. That's prospecting and sponsoring. Performing the right tasks at the right time is how you build a healthy business. Enthusiasm is a great business starter, but it takes discipline to be a stayer. You can't drive a network marketing business without taking consistent, purposeful actions—not only when it suits you, but all the time.

As you work the front line of your business, you'll get better at connecting and communicating with your customers, prospects, and team members. Your experiences will help you become a more empathetic leader, and your achievements will make you a more credible leader in the eyes of your team members.

No one who works, in or outside the home, expects to enjoy every task every day. But doing what we have to do, and not what we want to do, separates the warriors from the whiners in any business. You have to be willing to do what you need to do to get the results you want to get.

....

During my live presentations I often ask my audiences, "Who enjoys making calls?" Most confess that it's one of the least favorite tasks, and I invariably raise a laugh when I say, "There are only two types of network marketers: those who hate making calls, and liars."

But when you don't have enough appointments in your calendar, calling must be your top priority. If you don't have bookings you don't have a business.

> Doing the right things at the right time is how you grow. We pick
> up the phone because we have to, not because we want to.
> ●●●

There are many advantages to being your own boss, the best being that you're accountable only to yourself. But there are also challenges. When you dodge critical tasks you'll have to take the consequences. Your team members will suffer because they won't have a leader who sets an example they can follow.

You owe it to your team members to be the leader they deserve. Champions know that they must show up to go up, and they don't shirk their responsibilities to their customers, their team members, or themselves. They walk the talk, consciously and consistently. Their names appear often on the company's leader boards of top producers, and they're on stage at Conventions picking up the trophies.

Divide your time equally between personal activity and mentoring your team members. If you're not continually replenishing your personal group with personally sponsored team members you're taking two big risks:

First, if your team starts underperforming you won't meet the sales volume to maintain your status, or the bonuses that go with it.

Second, when your top performers become leaders in their own right, their distributors (and the distributors they sponsored) will now form a new "breakaway" group. When that happens, your personal group will take a hit. One of the most frequent causes of a drop in income comes from leaders who don't keep apace of their highest performers. All compensation plans require leaders to meet both a personal sales target and a personal group target before they are paid on the sales generated by breakaway groups.

●●●

A simple way to evaluate the strength of your personal group is to deduct the sales generated by your two top performers. Unless you can safely maintain the required sales without their sales, you need more team members. The fewer the number of people producing the volume you need to maintain your status, the more vulnerable your business is. The only security in any network marketing business is having the numbers.

Top network marketing leaders always have at least ten prospective team members on their radar. They understand the revolving-door nature of the business and they don't rely on anyone but themselves to maintain their status and rewards.

No matter how well your team members are (or aren't) performing, personal activity is the only part of your business you can completely control, and personal activity is how you show your team members that the business works—if you do!

Accomplish your personal targets before you tackle your team targets. Allocate the first half of the month for personal activity and the second half for mentoring your team.

Prioritizing your personal business does not mean neglecting your team members. They will learn more by your example than by explanation, and will trust a leader who has walked in their shoes.

Be a shining example to your team members by setting measurable monthly personal performance targets:

- I will earn the maximum commission for personal sales.
- I will sponsor a minimum of two new team members.
- I will exceed the minimum requirements to maintain my title.
- I will earn every incentive offered.

A champion knows the way and shows the way. Let your personal performance set the bar for your most ambitious team members! Motivate them with the message: *The only thing that excites me more than being number one each month is when one of you beats me!*

CHAPTER 8

Your Contacts List Is King!

A robust contacts list is one of the keys to a healthy network marketing business. Team members complaining, "I'm struggling to get appointments" should send chills down any leader's spine.

Network marketers whose calendars are blank are skirting dangerously close to the exit door. Their easiest option is always to quit, and most of them do. Half of all network marketers leave before the three-month mark, and four out of every five leave within a year.

There's a simple explanation for the high dropout rate. Most distributors jump-start their businesses through their inner circle of contacts. If they haven't mastered the art of creating new contacts before they exhaust supportive friends and family members, they will hit a brick wall in their businesses. The majority of them do not survive the crash.

Don't let that happen in your organization. Expanding their contacts and generating appointments should be one of the first skills new distributors master. Make it an integral component of your coaching program for new distributors, and a topic you review often with all team members. You may run out of appointments, but you're not out of the business if you still have people to contact.

••

Industry averages suggest that ten calls will lead to three appointments, which will lead to one new team member.

Three appointments a week would lead to 150 new connections a year. Introductions and referrals will multiply that number many times.

••

Set an example by becoming a champion of generating and keeping contacts. Here are fifteen strategies you can use to keep expanding your contact list:

1. Aim to add at least one new person to your contacts list each day. You can't keep working a stale list.

2. Make creating and maintaining new contacts a habit, like brushing your teeth. If you make ten calls a day, five days a week, you'll be making fifty connections a week.

3. Always have your antenna up for new contacts. If you're open, warm, and friendly you'll meet people everywhere you go.

4. Immediately capture new names from every event or encounter on your phone. A simple way to do it is to hand your phone over and say, "Put your name and number here so if you call me I'll know it's you." Send a text within twenty-four hours saying, "It was a pleasure meeting you," adding your first and last name to the text.

5. Regularly contact your contacts (they're called contacts for a reason!).

6. Don't be impatient for instant results. Relationships grow over time and with regular contact. Intersperse your sales calls with interesting news, tips, and information. Someone who is always in sales mode can become tiresome very quickly.

7. Make a follow-up call after every sale, and send a thank-you message every time a customer places an order through your online store. This is mandatory. Showing your appreciation is the way to elicit repeat business and referrals.

8. Treat your auto-ship or subscription customers as VIPs. Let them know how much you appreciate their loyalty. Ask for their feedback and check in monthly to inquire about their progress and offer encouragement. Send them regular tips and usage suggestions and invite them to special events such as a new product preview.

• •

Taking a subscription customer for granted is a fatal mistake. They are major targets for any other distributor promising a bigger, better, cheaper, or more scientifically credible product.

Loyalty is a fragile commodity. Give your preferred and auto-ship customers every reason to renew and no reason to cancel their subscription. Treat them the same as your team members. Make it easy for them to sign and hard for them to cancel by focusing on the relationship above and beyond everything else. Auto-ship customers are also your best source of introductions and referrals.

Industry-wide, the average period that auto-ship customers maintain their subscription is three months. If you're not giving them the red carpet treatment you will lose them.

• •

9. Spend more time in your local community. The greater your presence, the easier it will be to make new con-

nections. The more frequently people see you, the stronger their trust will be, especially if you show an interest in them long before you start trying to get them interested in you.

10. Let people know who you are, and how to find you. Turn your car into a moving billboard for your business. Always carry a stack of business cards, samples, and brochures.

11. If your contacts list is a mess, work on it for thirty minutes a day until it's fixed. Sloppy record keeping invariably leads to sloppy performance.

12. Think outside the box for ways to generate new contacts. Opportunities are everywhere. Sometimes you have to dig deep to find them.

••

Here's how three enterprising distributors addressed the challenge of creating contacts in communities with low populations.

One distributor in a farming town asked her rural delivery person to deliver welcome packages to all new families. The package included a couple of products, and her follow-up call was always warmly received.

A second distributor living in a small town encouraged everyone to host virtual parties for family and friends, and to order products for family and friends as gifts. As the company shipped direct to customers, it was a convenient and cost-effective way for her rural customers to shop.

A third distributor living in a remote mining township with a transitory population had the challenge of having to constantly generate new contacts. She created and advertised a weekly "Play in the Park" event where newcomers to town could bring their kids to meet other families informally. Her creativity paid off. Putting out the welcome mat for newcomers quickly led to new friendships and business. By holding the event in a public park she made it easy for people to show up. She alerted the press, and was featured in a front-page story in the local paper that was accompanied by a photo of the event. She also made the most of her situation to expand her business. When her clients settled in another city, her business gained roots there too.

Getting creative to generate contacts is not the sole domain of distributors in sparsely populated areas. One enterprising distributor went into her local electronics store, where the computers had Internet access, and loaded her business page onto all the screens. By the time she got home she had an order. When she phoned the customer to thank him it turned out to be a sales assistant who worked at the store, ordering gifts for his girlfriend's birthday.

When you factor in the potential of entering whole new circles of contacts, the reward for being resourceful is limitless.

13. Sponsor a junior sports team. Your investment will be small, but you are almost guaranteed to meet the parents. Being involved in family activities will demonstrate that you represent a family-first business more convincingly than any "we're a family-first business" tagline.

14. Ask for introductions and referrals. But be specific. If you are selling performance products, ask for an introduction to someone who works out, loves the outdoors, plays a sport, or is in training. But don't be clumsy. Offer a sample or trial, and ask for feedback. Take your time.

15. Add *and guest* to every social and business invitation. The more people you meet, the more money you will make.

How many people do you know? According to an article in the *New York Times*, the average person knows about 600 people. As making connections and building networks is what we do, most network marketers know many times that number.

Here are more than three hundred thought-starters to activate your brain cells into recalling how many people you know:

Accountant	Bible study group
Acquaintances	Bleachers
Active person	Blogger
Adult education classes	Bodybuilder
Aesthetician	Book club
Air Force	Border patrol
Armed Forces	Boss
Artist	Bridesmaids
Asks lots of questions	Bus driver
Assistants	Business center
Aunt	Business owners
Babysitter	Busy person
Baker	Butcher
Bank manager	Cake decorator
Bank officer	Car dealership
Barber	Carpet cleaner
Barista	Car service
Bar staff	Chamber of commerce
Beautician	Charity workers
Best friends	Checkout staff
Best man	Cheerleaders

Childhood friend

Chiropractor

Choir

Christmas card lists

Church members

Classmates

Cleaner

Club members

Coach

Coast Guard

College friends

Committee members

Community center

Computer technician

Condo

Counselor

Country club members

Course participants

Cousins

Coworkers

Craft club

Dance club

Daughter

Daughter-in-law

Day care

Delivery person

Dental hygienist

Dentist

Doctor

Dog walker

Drama club members

Drama coach

Dry cleaner

Electrician

Electrologist

Elocution tutor

Email list

Empty nester

Engaged

Entertainer

Enthusiast

Event planner

Everyone you meet

Exercise group

Facebook friends

Farmers' market

Fast-food workers

Father

Father-in-law

Favorite person

Fireman

First-home owner

Fitness coach

Flight attendant

Florist

Former customers

Former direct seller

Former hosts

Formerly in business

Former neighbors,
    associates, coworkers

Fraternity

Friendly person

Friends

Friends' friends

Fund-raising committee

Fun person

Furniture salesperson

Gardener

Girl Scout leader

Golf club

Government employee

Grandparents

Graph Search

Grocer

Groomsman

Groups I belong to

Guest lists

Gym instructor

Gym members

Hairdresser

Happy person

Hard worker

Health club

Health coach

Health enthusiast

Herbalist

High school friends

Holistic practitioner

Homemaker

Homeopath

Hospital

Hosts

Hotel receptionist

Housekeeper

House sitter

Housewife/husband

Husband's associates

Hygienist

Ice cream vendor

In debt

In-laws

Instagram

Insurance agent

Internet services

Janitor

Journalist

Karaoke
    acquaintances

Kids' contacts

Kindergarten

Knows everyone

Landlord	Massage therapist
Landscaper	Maternity ward
Language teacher	Mechanic
Laser technician	Midwife
Lawyer	Millennial
Librarian	Minister
Life coach	Mortgage broker
Lifeguard	Mother
Limo driver	Mother-in-law
Linked In contacts	Musician
Little League coach	Music teacher
Lives with parents	Nail salon
Loan officer	Nanny
Local retailer	Naturopath
Lollipop lady	Navy
Lost their job	Neighbor
Loves having fun	Nephew
Loves life	Newest friend
Loves my products	Newlywed
Loves to shop	New mom
Loves to travel	News media
Mail clerk	Niece
Mail delivery person	Night class student
Maintenance crew	Night class teacher
Manager	Nonprofit association staff
Manicurist	No-shows at previous party
Market stall	
Married couple	Nurse

Obstetrician

Old address book

Old school friends

Online connections

Optimist

Optometrist

Other direct sellers

Over the back fence

Owns a business

Pageant contestants

Pageant organizer

Parents of kids' friends

Parking attendant

Partners of coworkers
and associates

Part-time workers

Party guest

Passenger on my flight

Pastor

Pediatrician

Pediatric nurse

People I meet at the park

People who invite me
to their parties

Performer

Personal trainer

Pet groomer

Pet sitter

Pet walker

Pharmacist

Phone contacts

Photographer

Photo shop assistant

Physiotherapist

Pizza delivery

Playgroup moms

Plumber

Police officer

Post office worker

Pregnant

Professor

PTA committee

Qualities I admire

Queues or people
I meet in line

Rabbi

Radiologist

Realtor

Receptionists

Relatives

Reporter

Retailers

Retired

Room service
staff

Salesclerk

School friends

School staff

Scoutmaster

Security staff

Server

Service clubs

Service provider

Shared interests

Shoe repair

Shopper

Siblings

Single parent

Sister

Sister-in-law

Social circle

Social clubs

Social media

Someone you just met

Sorority

Spa

Spanish teacher

Sporting contacts

Starbucks

Stay-at-home mom

Stepbrother

Stepsister

Students from high school, college, graduate school

Successful person

Supervisor

Swim instructor

Tailor

Talented person

Talkative person

Tanning salon

Taxi driver

Tax professional

Teacher

Teacher's aide

Temple

Tenant

Tennis coach

Therapist

Thrift store

Toastmasters

Tradesperson

Trash collector

Traveler

Tutor

Twitter

Uberdriver

Uncles

University classmates

Uses similar products

Vacation friends and
acquaintances

Vacation home
neighbors

Valet parking
attendant

Vendor

Veterinarian

VIP customers

VIP hosts

Voice coach

Volunteer

Waiter

Walking group

Walks by my house

Waxing technician

Wedding guests

Wedding planner

Weight loss coach and
support group
members

Wives of my coworkers
and associates

Wives of my husband's
friends and associates

X-ray technician

Yearbook

Yoga teacher

Youthful person

Youth group leader

YouTube

Zany person

Zoo staff

CHAPTER **9**

Maximizing the Potential of Social Media

Social media has brought the biggest boon to network marketers since the industry began, offering unlimited access to a mind-boggling array of contacts.

When I helped an American company launch into Australia in 2013 and 2014 I conducted a survey among the first five hundred people to sign on, to find out where they first heard about the company.

Apart from the traditional methods, such as being invited, introduced, or referred by someone they knew, the reports included meeting on *Star Wars* and *Candy Crush* fan pages, having babies on the same day, and sharing a birthday or last name.

Some sponsors found their first distributors by joining social networking sites and others by starting social networking sites. The message is clear: You can never really know what's going to work so try everything.

These seven basics steps will help you maximize the potential of social media:

1. Find out where your potential contacts are on social media and join them there. If they move elsewhere, follow them.

2. Make it easy for former and new contacts to find you by sharing as much information as possible on your sites, while protecting sensitive details.

3. Make sure your Facebook page instantly identifies the company you work with. When people check you out they will know they have come to the right place.

4. Give your contacts a reason to follow you on your social media pages:
   - A lively newsfeed of information and ideas
   - Inspirational affirmations, quotes, and video clips
   - Key benefits of popular products and services

5. Send friend requests to every person you meet with a friendly message that will remind them who you are and how you met. Take a few minutes before you send your message to look for common interests to incorporate into your message. For example, "I'm also a Giants fan." Don't try to sell them anything. This is not the time for a buy/book/business message unless you want to come across as a jerk.

6. Use Facebook's Graph Search feature to search for people with similar interests, backgrounds, and circumstances. For example, classmates who graduated the same year, have similar hobbies, or like the things you like.

7. Do your homework. Social media is not an open invitation to become an online predator.

   Here is an example of what not to do: *Dear Mary, Would you mind listening to the three-minute call that*

I just recorded, and give me your feedback. I would greatly appreciate it, because I am very excited about this opportunity.

This is an exact copy of a message I received, but I get several similar approaches a week via my LinkedIn and Facebook accounts. What's missing? Two things, for starters:

1. The writer has made no attempt to learn anything about me.

2. The writer has made no attempt to connect with me.

Such a careless approach is inexcusable when you consider how much the senders would find out with a simple two-minute search.

I asked Karen Clark, a social media expert and owner of My Business Presence, to share her best strategies for increasing your visibility on social media. These are her top recommendations:

1. *Find great keywords.* Think about the words or phrases your prospects will type into their search engines to describe the problems they're having or solutions they're seeking. Using those words will make it easy for them to find you. The closer the match between the words you're using and they're using, the more people you'll find. If you're unsure where to start, there are many free keyword research tools on the Web that will help you.

2. *Make the most of your "About" page.* Most social media sites provide room for you to describe your business, your products, and your services. Use the space to share your personal story and what drew you to the business. The more people know about you the more they will trust you, and your story will provide more

words for the search engines to match you to prospects.

3. *Use a great headshot.* Your profile picture may be the first impression visitors will have of you and your business. Use a clear image with nothing distracting in the background, and crop your image to fit the space. Half a headshot is not a good look.

4. *Be visually consistent.* Use similar images across all your social media platforms so that you are easily recognizable. And don't forget to follow your company's policies about image creation, personal branding, and use of the company logo.

5. *Focus on one site.* You'll get better results if you build a strong presence on one social media site than if you try to cover too many. If you have accounts on multiple sites, cross-post occasionally. If you stop getting results, it may be a sign that your prospects have moved elsewhere. If all else fails, ask them.

6. *Use a business page.* Whenever you have an option to do so, use a public business page. Business pages are typically set to be public by default, and that means every message, image, and caption you post will be indexed by one of the search engines. Business pages also make it easy for your connections to "like" or "follow" you.

7. *Wait and see with new social media.* When new sites come out, secure an account with your chosen username and then adopt a "wait and see" approach. You don't have to jump in and start participating immediately. Let the developers work out the glitches and kinks that invariably occur in the first six months while you stay focused on what's working for you today.

8. *Take it off-line.* Start a private conversation when someone seems interested, but don't move too soon. Watch for green flags, such as asking questions, consistently engaging, or requesting more information. When people appear to be truly interested, privately message them to ask for permission to email or call. If at any point you get pushback from your online prospect let it go. When the timing is right you can try again.

9. *Post mostly nonmarketing messages.* Your posts should offer more than marketing messages about your products, services, or opportunity. I suggest that you aim for 90 percent of your content to be on related side topics. When you do market your business, your readers will be more likely to click your link or share your post because they trust you. Letting everyone benefit from your posts whether or not they do business with you helps builds rapport, trust, and loyalty.

10. *Use social media CPR: Comment-Post-Reply.* Take time to comment on posts from your connections. Post consistently to build up your visibility. Reply to comments or questions directed to you. Try to be the last reply in a thread of comments on your page by revisiting your posts at the end of the day and adding to the conversation. This shows your readers that you are hands-on, which will encourage them to engage with you.

11. *Do not overpost.* The acceptable amount to post varies by social media platform. Observe the culture of each site, and behave accordingly. For example, LinkedIn moves fairly slowly, so one or two posts per week are fine. Facebook readers tend to tolerate between one and three posts per day. More than that and you risk

being flagged for spam. Twitter requires multiple post-ings per day, as readers are exposed only to posts that are live when they log in.

12. *Type conversationally.* Your best posts will come from the heart. Don't get so caught up in the mechanics of writing that you hinder your ability to communicate person-to-person. Think about how you would convey your thoughts to somebody in person, and post the same way. Using the built-in dictation app on your smartphone to compose social media posts is a good option to keep your style real.

13. *Teach something.* Think of yourself as a resource cen-ter where people can go to learn. Apart from your products and opportunity, look for other places where you can build your reputation as an expert by sharing ideas, how-to tips, information, and articles. People will look forward to reading your posts if they learn something that benefits their lives.

14. *Be yourself.* Trust is everything. Be someone people will want to do business with online and off. Think of social media as the virtual you. If you attended a net-working event in your community, how would you be-have? Would you pass your business cards out to everyone, and ask everyone to buy your products or join your team? I hope not! The same is true for social media. If you blast promotional messages at every turn, people will tune you out; "unfollow" you; or, worse mark you as spam. Before you post anything, ask your-self, "Would I say this in real life?"

15. *Be interactive.* Add value to other people's conversa-tions. The more you interact with their content, the more they will get to know you. You will also gain vis-ibility within their network, which will include people

you have not yet met. People love it when you notice them. Liking, commenting on, or "favoriting" other people's posts is appreciated. Consider interacting with people you would like to notice you, too.

16. *Follow corporate guidelines.* Always follow your company policies for compliance in branding, naming your profiles/pages, and messaging. It's your responsibility as an independent business owner to read your company's Internet marketing, advertising, and social media policies and procedures. The policies are designed to protect you and the corporate identity.

17. *Follow all federal and state laws.* It's important that your marketing messages comply with the law. The Federal Trade Commission and other organizations monitor social media posts for compliance. Specific public disclosures must be included if you're making health claims or statements about income, for example. Contact your company if you don't understand the requirements and keep abreast of the latest updates by researching government agencies and "dot-com disclosures."

18. *Follow site-specific terms.* Avoid having your accounts restricted. When you join social media sites you agree to the terms of service. Most people do not read the fine print, but as a business owner, it's your responsibility to read the terms of service that you agreed to, as well as updates that occur later. Social media sites have the right to withdraw your account at any time and for any reason. If you are not following the rules, you are putting your business at risk.

19. *Secure image rights.* When you're using images in your posts make sure you have a right to do so. It is a common misperception that images that can be found

freely on the Internet are "fair use" to use any way you like. This is not true. The originator of the image owns the copyright. The only way you can be certain that you have a right to use an image is to take the picture yourself, or acquire it from a royalty-free image site and include proper attribution.

20. *Monitor your privacy.* Social media sites often start out with one set of privacy rules and then change them. Check your privacy settings every six months. For example, you might not want your personal phone number to be visible to the public, but you want your website and business email visible. You may want to keep the month and day you were born public so that your social media friends can wish you a happy birthday, but keep your year of birth private to protect yourself against identity theft.

Social Advertising
Jim Lupkin and Brian Carter,
Authors, *Network Marketing for Facebook*

Social advertising has opened up a whole new playing field for network marketers. Apart from using social media to connect and communicate, it offers a new way to generate contacts. With social advertising you can cost-effectively target a specific market, with ads costing as little as a dollar a day.

Before you start social advertising, decide what your goal is. The more specific you are, the more successful your ads will be. For example, do you want to raise awareness, generate leads, grow fans and followers, make sales, get more samples of your product out, or raise attendance for a local event?

Next, decide which platform you will use. Facebook is currently the best platform because it has the most users and features, and offers the best targeting. It is also the most affordable advertising option for raising awareness and generating leads.

Facebook ads are a good place to start for anyone venturing for the first time into Facebook advertising. The success of Facebook ads comes down to a combination of targeting, image, headline, and body copy. Try to create a website conversion ad to get leads or sales. Our experience suggests that they don't work as well for bottom-line results.

The cost of Twitter ads can be high, but Twitter has advantages. Lead cards make it easier for people to opt in, which leads to high conversion rates.

LinkedIn ads tend to be limited. The basic LinkedIn ads are small and often missed by users, which makes it difficult to get many clicks. It can cost several thousand dollars a month to get access to enhanced ads.

YouTube ads can be created via AdWords. Run your video as an advertisement before other videos. If people skip it, you pay nothing. If they watch it you pay about ten cents per view.

The benefit of social media advertising is that you can create ads and then test them, making adjustments and improvements based on the results you are achieving. The way to get great results is to test a lot of ads.

The first aspect to test is targeting. Use a matter-of-fact description of your offering and a logo. You're doing a somewhat boring ad on purpose. Test interest targeting, demographics, and behaviors separately—one ad per ad set, in three to five ad sets.

Once you find the best targets, test multiple images and headlines to get even better results. Here's where you get into more exciting images and copywriting. When you get a higher click response from the ad, Facebook usually rewards you with lower costs.

Facebook is built around positivity and likes. The best images are close-up, happy faces. People also love babies, animals, and humor. Search for horizontally oriented Shutterstock images, as you can use them at no cost within your Facebook ads.

When you are creating copy, talk about how your product offering will help your target audience. Don't bring up a negative topic unless your product is designed to solve the problem. Find a way of describing your product that positively resonates with your audience's need.

If you keep testing, you'll keep improving.

CHAPTER 10

Use Trade Shows and Events to Expand Your Prospect Pool

It's better to take a proactive approach to ensuring a flow of fresh faces into your organization than to wait until your leads have dried up. There is no greater security for your business than having a reservoir of prospects to call. With untapped leads in your reservoir you avoid having to scroll through the same list looking for someone to call. We all know what a demoralizing experience that can be.

There's no better place to gain experience at expanding your contacts than vendor events. You'll be competing against other vendors to attract the best prospects, so they provide the perfect arena for sharpening your prospecting skills.

Vendor events offer more than an opportunity to replenish your contacts; they diversify your prospects. The more diverse your prospects are the better chance you have to branch out into new circles of contacts. By doing several trade shows, fairs, farmers' markets, or vendor events a year, you will elevate your business to a whole new level of visibility.

The quantity of contacts you generate online may be greater but not the quality. When it comes to connecting, nothing can replace the magic of face-to-face. Even if you are a skilled online prospector, your growth strategy should include creating contacts at events.

Don't restrict yourself to your hometown. The highest earners constantly seek to widen their horizons, and they never hesitate to enter new territories. Decide how far you are willing or able to travel, make a list of possible places within that area, and start searching online for vendor events.

Get creative by booking events that less-imaginative competitors may overlook. Put yourself among young people at a college open day, a concert, sporting event, or street festival. Meet women by setting up shop at a gun show, car show, truck show, or boat show. They may be attending to support their spouses, and will welcome a chance to talk about something different. The same applies to targeting men. You can almost guarantee their attention at an event that is predominantly geared to women.

Contact your local chamber of commerce, city hall, sports organizations, churches, and schools and ask for their event calendars. By going direct, you set yourself ahead of less-determined competitors. The most useful function on your mobile device is still the phone.

Try to make personal contact with the event organizer if possible. You'll be networking with the most connected person at the event.

A good rule to follow for events is look for quality over quantity. You will fare better by aiming to connect with a few good prospects than collecting a bunch of random phone numbers.

One of the keys to maximizing vendor events is not sacrificing long-term opportunities for short-term rewards. While you are absorbed in trying to close a sale, a potential team member may wander in and out of your booth. My experiences have proved over and over that many network marketers have close encounters with prospects without realizing it.

You are using your product as your draw card, but your purpose must always be business. Put your focus on sponsoring. When you let prospects walk by you can be sure they will find a home with someone else.

You have a much better chance of starting a conversation with a simple "What brought you here today?" than a ham-fisted "Have you heard of [company name]?" It's not only a tired-out cliché, it leads precisely nowhere. Your opener is your best and possibly only chance to start a conversation. People never tire of their favorite topic: themselves!

You'll fare better by showing an interest in others than by trying to make them interested in you. Relax, have fun, and be generous with help, support, and genuine compliments.

Lucky draw slips are as unimaginative as they are outdated. Most of the contacts will give you their details with the sole purpose of winning the prize you are offering. There is every chance they will not welcome your "You didn't win but I can offer you a free consultation" call. This can be especially disheartening for rookies, so it's not a good example to set.

Trade shows can be expensive and time consuming. If they're worth doing, they're worth doing well. These strategies will help you make the most of every vendor event:

1. Invest in good, portable signage that you can use over and over again.

2. Create an eye-catching display that is not crowded with products. Make your business opportunity prominent.

3. Take new team members with you. They will learn a lot by observing you in action. If the event is a large one, consider making it a team event.

4. Aim to be the best dressed at the event. This could be anything from a suit and tie if you are offering professional services to a T-shirt with a company logo.

• •

Being best dressed is being appropriately dressed. Your aim is to connect, not impress. At a weekend family event most attendees will be casually dressed. A suit and tie may look out of place whereas by wearing a fashionable, open-neck shirt under a tailored jacket you will come across as professional and approachable. The same principle applies when you visit a client's or prospect's home. The first key to connecting is that the person feels comfortable and relaxed with you.

• •

5. If your product begs to be demonstrated, create an interactive booth that will draw people in. Samples and demonstrations are easy examples, but there are many ways to attract and engage visitors to your booth, such as:
   • A sixty-second health analysis for nutritional products
   • A sixty-second financial checkup for financial services

6. People are always more convinced by things they discover for themselves. Fun self-revealing "questionnaires" will tell you what you need to know to engage with future clients and recruits. Here is an example of a sixty-second questionnaire that will gauge the potential of future team members. If possible, do it with them so that you can start building a connection.

Rate My Job!

❏ I'm paid what I'm worth.

❏ I get an annual pay increase.

❏ I set my own hours.

❏ I am appreciated for my contribution.

❏ The company pays for my annual vacation.

❏ I receive unlimited training.

❏ I'm invited to the company's annual Convention.

❏ I can take time off to attend to personal or family matters.

❏ I like the people I work with.

❏ I enjoy going to work each day.

❏ My job is secure.

❏ My income covers all my expenses.*

Too many unchecked boxes? Maybe it's time to consider starting your own business!

* Identifying a gap between their income and expenses will help you segue into talking about a part-time business.

7. The trickiest part of the prospecting process is often getting your prospect to take the second step. Amateurs are impulsive. They hotly pursue anyone who crosses their path. This approach seldom leads to the higher incomes, and even more rarely leads to sustainable success. Leaders are intuitive. They know when to advance, when to wait, and when to back off.

The more relaxed you are about a meeting or invitation to an upcoming event, the less likely it is that your prospect will sense pressure. For example:

"Do you have time for a quick coffee this week?"

"How about I drop by your house one night this week?"

"We're hosting an informal event next week. Would you like to come? You're welcome to bring someone with you."

The more vendor events you do, the more skilled you will become at connecting with prospects. While most vendors will show up, set up, and hope people will stop by their booth, leaders have a clear strategy for maximizing their time and financial investment.

CHAPTER 11

Sponsoring Wide and Deep

Most of us believe that the impact we make on the world matters, and through your business you'll have countless opportunities to enrich other people's lives. You'll do it by sharing your business with the same passion and focus as you share your products.

Many will say they're not interested, too busy, or don't like network marketing, and that's fine. You don't need everyone. But if you believe in your business, you'll invite everyone without second guessing the responses.

You cannot build a network marketing business alone. It takes an army to reach the highest incomes, and nothing will add more instant and potentially lasting value to your business than a new team member.

> Residual income is the reward you receive
> tomorrow for the work you do today.

Statistically, new people tend to be the highest producers, and they are bursting with potential. They, or someone they sponsor, could bring your next shining star on board.

There are countless network marketing opportunities for your future team members to choose from and thousands of ambitious, aspiring leaders targeting the same people as you. To attract and keep the best people you have to be at the top of your game.

Momentum is everything. You won't build a sustainable team without empathy, or by using high-pressure techniques, but you need to create a system that works, and then confidently and consistently work that system.

A haphazard approach will lead to haphazard results and will be impossible for your team members to duplicate. Instead of simply following your proven system, they will be stumbling around trying to create their own strategy. Duplication is the key to building your team fast and deep!

....

The term *deep* is used in network marketing to refer to recruits who are introduced to your organization by your recruits. Personally sponsored recruits become your "first levels" and give your team "width." Their personally sponsored recruits become your "second levels," and that is how your team gains depth.

The people they sponsor become your "third levels" and so on. The way to build a business that produces a steady stream of residual income is to build your team wide by personally sponsoring, and deep by encouraging and training your people to recruit. It's the combination of width and depth that creates a stable, sustainable network marketing business.

....

Incorporate these core techniques into your sponsoring system and perform them over and over until they become second nature. When you're confidently and consistently sponsoring, your example will inspire your team members to sponsor.

Develop a Sponsoring Mindset

Every good network marketing business is built around great products, but don't let the short-term satisfaction of selling distract you from the long-term rewards of sponsoring. Selling is a job. Sponsoring makes it a business. Take your business materials with you everywhere (leaving them in the car when you're working out at the gym is not taking them everywhere).

> Sales are your income for today,
> appointments are your income for tomorrow,
> sponsoring is your income forever.

Share Your Business Opportunity at Every Appointment, Presentation, and Event

Weave sponsoring references throughout every conversation and every presentation! If you need prompting, place discreet stickers on a few products or brochures to remind you that it's time to pitch the business! The more practice you get, the easier you'll find it to segue the conversation from selling to sponsoring.

You're looking for people who are perfect for your business because your business is perfect for them. You don't need everyone but you ask everyone because you'll never know who is interested until and unless you ask.

No matter how deep you have to dig to find the courage to ask, it will always be less painful than discovering that someone you didn't approach when you had the chance signed with someone else. Offer the opportunity to everyone and let each person decide whether to accept or decline your offer.

Stop *Hoping* to Meet Your Next Team Member at Presentations and Events

Tell yourself instead: *I know my next recruit is here. I just have to work out who it is.* This minor attitude shift gave my business a major boost. It shifted my focus away from my own stage fright to identifying my next team member.

Your Customers Will Always Be Your Best Prospects

They're using the product, which means they're practically knocking on the door to becoming distributors. The same applies to hosts of party plan consultants. Picture them as being in a "VIP new team member waiting area" and give them your best customer experience. When the timing is right, ask them to upgrade to becoming a distributor. The more rewarding their experience as a customer, the more open they'll be to a business presentation.

Auto-Ship or Subscription Customers Are Only a Short Step Away from Becoming Distributors

If you keep your message casual when you approach them you'll make it easier for them to make the transition: "You're already saving money on your own products. Why not make a few dollars sharing them with your friends? Of everyone you know, who is most likely to be interested in [losing a few pounds, going on a wellness program]?" With this approach you're also inviting them to think about their first customers.

Always Keep Your Antenna Up for Potential Team Members

If you're not always on high alert you could easily miss their signals. They won't all be sending out strong signals, and that's where inexperienced recruiters let top prospects walk by without noticing them.

Leaders don't make superficial judgments, or lock themselves into first impressions. They appreciate that many people choose not to show what they're thinking until they're ready to do so. They learn to watch for the weaker, more subtle signals that most people miss. Develop a habit of thinking:

- Who will be interested?
- Why will they be interested?

Create your own clue-cards that will alert you when you meet people who fit the profile of network marketer. For my book *Be a Recruiting Superstar* I researched tens of thousands of network marketers from hundreds of companies to identify who is most likely to join. My research indicated that these groups are over-whelmingly more open to an approach about the business:

- Moms eager to raise their families without giving up their two-income lifestyle.

- Students wanting a head start in business while they're still studying.

- Couples who dream of being partners at home and work. My experience tells me that the younger they are, the more likely couples will want to share income and family responsibilities equally.

- Workers looking for a way to supplement their modest nine-to-five paycheck to enhance their lifestyle. The chance to travel has motivated many people to moon-light as network marketers.

- Professional practitioners (especially the medical, sports, fitness, beauty, wellness, and personal growth fields) seeking a product line that will complement their consulting business, provide a second income source, or set up a residual income stream for when they are no longer consulting.

- Younger people willing to take a risk or two to follow their dreams. Millennials are your future organization and they're hungry for entrepreneurial opportunities. They have never aspired to the lifestyle their parents re-signed themselves to when career options were more limited. Nor do they have any intention of spending the next forty years letting someone else dictate the terms by which they work. They're primed and impatient for a better way to fund their lifestyle today and their dreams for tomorrow. They also have fewer financial responsibilities, which gives them more freedom to choose what they want to do. According to a Pew Research Center analysis of the most recent U.S. Census Bureau data, 36 percent of America's young adults aged between eighteen and thirty-one are still living with their parents. They can afford to take a short-term risk to pursue a long-term reward. I see a neon O-P-P-O-R-T-U-N-I-T-Y sign flashing right there!

....

Be a Recruiting Superstar identifies a predominance of the following key target groups among the highest income earners:

- Teachers

- Current customers and clients

- Engineers

- Hosts

- Nurses

- Creative people

- Moms

- Millennials

- Former network marketers

....

Think Positively

When you offer prospects the business you're inviting them into your community. That's paying them a compliment, so don't over-think it. If they decline, say something like: "I'm sure someone like you is approached all the time." Closing with a compliment defuses the discomfort and you'll both feel better.

Take Ownership of Your Sponsoring Success Rate

If you're not consistently sponsoring there can be only one of three reasons:

- You're not offering the business to enough people.

- You're offering the business to the wrong people.

- You're using the wrong approach.

If you're not getting lots of "No's," you're not approaching enough people. Instead of fretting that they'll say no, give them a chance to say no. We'd all prefer to be given the chance to decline than not be invited. A few will say yes, some will say maybe, and lots will say no. Work the numbers. The *only* guaranteed way to fail is not to ask!

Don't let impatience be your downfall. If you make a move too soon or come on too strong you'll succeed only at scaring them away. Prospecting is a little like dating. If you're smart you'll keep it casual until you've made a connection, and then take it slow to give the relationship time to develop. Never back your prospects into a wall.

Don't dominate the conversation, no matter how passionate you are about your opportunity. The more interaction you have with prospects, the easier it will be to identify potential team members. When you're doing most of the talking you'll come across as pushy or desperate. All great recruiters understand the power of patience.

No One Wants to Be Ambushed by a Mindless Sponsoring Pitch

Think before you speak: *Do I know enough about this person's wants or needs to credibly offer her the business?* If you don't know what she wants, how can you provide an answer? Take a step back and work on the relationship.

Always Be Prepared with Your Best Offer

At the start of each month, check for any "Join Now" incentives your company is offering, such as discounts, free kit upgrades, extra Fast-Start rewards. The start of an incentive trip qualification period can also be a good time to generate a little "now is the time" urgency. But don't overplay your hand. Pressure is a huge turnoff to prospects. You may find a few spontaneous personalities who respond impulsively but most people appreciate being given time to consider their decision.

Tell Prospects Why You Want Them on Your Team

Make your prospects feel good about joining you by making them feel good about themselves. A sincere compliment is the perfect pathway to talking business.

- *You're always upbeat. I know I would enjoy working with you.*

- *You would be a great asset to our business.*

- *You're one of my best clients. I can't help thinking what a great distributor you would make.*

- *The results you've achieved would impress anyone. Have you thought about turning your experiences into a business?*

There's No Such Thing as a One-Size-Fits-All Pitch!

You have to adapt your approach to fit your prospect's personality. Enthusiastic Peacocks will respond to compliments and the fun, social aspect of network marketing. Analytical Owls will want facts and figures, and expect accurate responses to their questions. Be direct and businesslike with competitive Eagles, as they won't respect hesitation. Give conservative Doves space to make a decision and let insecure Swans know that you are willing to mentor them.

You will learn more about the nuances of different personalities and how to approach them in my book *Be a Direct Selling Superstar.*

Look for People Who Want Money Rather Than Those Who Need It

It's not what we need, it's what we want that drives us, and you can waste a lot of time trying to help people who aren't motivated to change their own lives. Build your organization with doers, not dreamers.

It's the gap between what we have and what we want that motivates us! Make a habit of asking targeted questions to identify what's missing in your prospect's life:

- *Would you describe yourself as a spender or a saver?*

- *If you had $1,000 in your wallet right now, what would you spend it on?*

- *If you were given a $100 a week pay raise what would you do with it?*

- *If you could make one big purchase this year, what would it be?*

Stop Informing and Start Inspiring

Emotion packs more power than facts and figures. Introduce your business by sharing your story and experiences. You'll know if your prospects are responding by the signals they're sending.

- Are they maintaining eye contact?

- Are their eyes lighting up?

- Are they nodding?

- Are they smiling?

If not, chances are they already switched to sleep mode.

Don't race ahead of yourself. Most of your prospects will not be thinking about the business. Your first challenge is to light a spark that inspires them to start thinking about it.

What lights a fire in one prospect won't necessarily ignite another. Learn to create sparks that highlight a variety of social, emotional, and financial benefits of the business. No matter how bright the spark is, it won't light a fire if it misses your prospect's hot spot.

Make It Easy for Prospects to Say Yes

The message that you can keep your full-time job while building a business in your spare time will appeal to anyone who is unwilling or unable to give up a regular income. It also shortens the step toward signing.

Many workers want to maintain the security of their regular incomes while testing the waters before making a big leap into self-employment. An overwhelming majority of network marketers enter the business as part-time entrepreneurs, or with small or short-terms goals that explode when they experience firsthand how fulfilling and rewarding it can be.

Nonetheless, don't assume that prospects are interested in working their businesses only part-time. Some will be in a stronger position to work their businesses full-time from the start. For example, it may be that:

- Your company offers financial support during the first months as part of their orientation and training program.

- You are approaching young people who have yet to start earning and can camp in their parents' home while they build a business.

- Your prospects have sufficient savings to tide them over until the paychecks start flowing.

- Your prospects are a working couple who can afford to give up one income to build a business that may ultimately replace both incomes.

That's where the power of asking the right questions comes in. The more you ask, the more you'll know how to position the business to meet each prospect's unique circumstances and expectations.

Market Yourself Every Day

Being courteous, professional, and interested in others in all your dealings will make a positive impression on everyone you meet. When they think of someone they would love to do business with, they will think of you!

Don't waste time chasing a reluctant recruit just because you think he'd be good at it. This business isn't for everyone. If you have to convince someone, he's not the right person.

Lose Your Fear of Rejection

Rejection is part of the process of sifting through your prospects to find the positive, enthusiastic people who will recognize the amazing opportunity you're offering them. They're not saying no to you—they're saying no to the business.

Create a Sponsoring Culture in Your Organization

You can do this if you:

- Keep the message alive by talking about sponsoring consistently and confidently.

- Personally sponsor a minimum of two new team members every month.

- Coach every team member to answer these questions persuasively in fifteen seconds or less:
    - What inspired you to join?
    - What inspires you now?

- Feed team members a constant source of suggestions, tips, and techniques.

- Encourage new people to start sponsoring immediately. Use the new distributor rewards in your compensation plan to focus them on finding and signing their first recruit. If they question why they should sponsor say: "Sponsoring opens up a whole new way for you to generate income. Why not take advantage of everything you can earn?"

It may help to ask them to imagine they have earned a free vacation and can take anyone except their partner or children with them. Ask: "Who would you take with you? Who can you see yourself having the most fun with?" Suggest that they call that person and invite him or her to join so they can support each other.

- Create a sense of urgency and excitement by running impromptu, "Do It Now" sponsoring challenges. You'll find that a forty-eight-hour sponsoring challenge will inspire instant action, whereas a longer incentive may encourage them to procrastinate. Get them motivated by saying: "You already know your next recruit. All you have to do is work out who it is and contact that person." Your certainty will help to boost their courage and confidence.

- Constantly remind your team members: "They're not saying no to you. They're saying no to the business."

- Encourage every team member to read *Be a Recruiting Superstar*.

• •

Start a *Be a Recruiting Superstar* book club. The process is simple:

- Promote the book club throughout your organization with a starting date that gives everyone a chance to obtain a personal copy of the book.

- Set up a closed Facebook group as a forum for participants to share their stories and successes.

- Encourage them to read one chapter a week.

- Follow each chapter with a challenge to apply what they learn. For example, "Identify and approach someone who fits the description in this week's chapter."

- Encourage participants to share:
  - What did I learn from the current chapter?
  - How will I act on what I learned?

- Keep participants energized and excited by celebrating all those who recruited that week and inviting them to share how they did it.

- Add to the excitement by aligning your book club to a current corporate incentive. For example, "Sign up ten qualified recruits,* and you'll be winging your way to a luxury resort in the Bahamas."

*Most if not all companies stipulate that new recruits achieve a minimum sales target for their sponsor to qualify for sponsoring incentives.

Above All, Look for People You Would Like to Surround Yourself With

When your business goes as well as you plan, you will be spending a lot of time with team members. Make sure prospects seem to be a good fit with you and your organization.

PART THREE

Learn to Communicate

CHAPTER 12

Effective Communication Is Job #1

Consistent, high-impact messaging will always be one of your most powerful business-building tools. You become a leader by inspiring your prospects to join you in the business. You grow as a leader by inspiring them to work their businesses. The more persuasive a communicator you are, the more influence you will have on your team's performance.

Your income could depend on how well you communicate.

Earlier in this book I explained that you start your business with the strengths you have, and develop the strengths you need as you progress. Learning to communicate effectively should be at the top of your list of personal growth initiatives. The sooner you learn to be a persuasive communicator, the sooner you will reach the higher-income levels.

Leaders don't communicate to disseminate information. They communicate to inspire, excite, and energize people into action. They know that belief and vision carry more firepower than facts and figures. Whether they're addressing one person or a multitude, their confidence, belief, and optimism shine through all their communications.

We do what we are inspired to do,
not what we're told to do!

One of the truest tests of a persuasive communicator is how intensely you engage your audiences. Getting their attention is not enough. They may be listening to be polite, or because they can't discreetly leave. That doesn't mean they're engaged. They're engaged when they're thinking about what you are saying; responding to what you're saying; and, more important, responding to you.

You won't become a powerful communicator overnight. But you can start small and power up your presentations gradually by accepting every invitation to make a live presentation. These steps will help you deliver persuasive presentations every time, whether your audience is one or a thousand.

Step One: Let Your Audiences' Circumstances, Experiences, and Interests Guide Your Content and Your Delivery
The people you're speaking to hold all the power. They can tune in or tune out at any time. Before you start talking, think: Whom am I talking to? Why should they care? If you don't know, find out. If you're in a one-on-one situation start by asking questions. If you're speaking to a group, do your research. Even the most powerful messages will miss the mark if they're directed at the wrong audience.

Anyone can sell to someone who's already interested, but only the most persuasive communicators turn "maybes" into "yeses," small orders into large orders, customers into distributors, and distributors into leaders.

Step Two: Prepare Your Presentations by Starting at the End and Working Backward
Consider:

*   How do you want them to think?

- How do you want them to feel?
- What do you want them to do?

When you have established the outcome you want, you can plan how you will take your audience there. The most effective presentations focus on making one key point and bringing it to life with stories, anecdotes, and examples. If you present a laundry list of points your key message may get lost.

Step Three: Aim to Reach Your Audience's Hearts as Well as Their Heads

If you're not touching your audiences emotionally you're not connecting. When you speak from the heart your presentations will become more meaningful and memorable.

Throughout my career as a speaker I have listened to thousands of speakers. What distinguishes the best from the rest is simple. They care deeply about making a difference in their audience's lives. When you care about your audience you will automatically speak from the heart.

Step Four: Slow Down! Give Your Audience Time to Think

When you talk too fast, your audience has no time to digest what you're saying. When you talk for too long they'll have no chance to respond. If you subject them to a torrent of words they will become confused or disengaged.

Never use more words than you need, and remember to pause often. What will feel like a long pause to you will appear all too brief to your audience.

> Simplicity is the ultimate sophistication.
> LEONARDO DA VINCI

When you speak less, people will listen more. When you listen more, you'll learn more. You'll know exactly what your audience wants to hear, and you won't waste your time or theirs with superfluous information. No one has the time or the patience to listen to waffle, so every point must pack a punch. Wordiness is a sign of arrogance; your audiences deserve better.

Step Five: Don't Let Your Fears Handicap You

When I first started speaking I was almost paralyzed by nerves. I still remember the humiliation I felt when I stood up to speak and nothing came out. To overcome my nerves I joined a Toastmasters club. It took years to become comfortable speaking in public, but if I had allowed my fear to consume me, I would not have the life I have today. It takes courage, not confidence, to pursue the life you dream about.

Step Six: Don't Provoke or Offend People

Safeguard your image as a professional and avoid saying or writing anything contentious. Even one person offended is one person too many.

I learned this lesson the hard way. I was speaking to an audience that was predominantly moms and making the point that while our talent for multitasking serves us well when it comes to managing the myriad of household tasks we perform each day, it can sabotage our success in business. By trying to do more we often end up achieving less.

For fun, I added that the pendulum swings at home when we try to persuade our husbands to multitask. If we ask them to put out the trash and feed the dog, their most likely response will be, "Which one do you want me to do?"

One of the few men in the audience complained to the company that my comments were offensive to men. Although most of the audience gave my presentation positive reviews I lost any chance of a callback. It was a harsh way to learn to be more careful about how I illustrate my *Don't try to be Wonder Woman* point.

Step Seven: Pronounce Names Correctly

If in doubt, ask, and then make a note so you don't have to ask again. I cringe when I hear corporate executives who are publicly recognizing achievers trying to guess how to pronounce a name. It's a huge insult to the recipient and could spoil an otherwise momentous occasion in his or her life.

You can avoid such insensitivity by a simple process called preparation. Imagine the thrill you would feel if someone called you to check on how your name is pronounced, or whether you prefer to use your full name, say Catherine, or the shortened version Cathy. What better way to make someone feel special? I can't say this enough: It's the small gestures that reveal our true selves.

Step Eight: Avoid Using Abbreviations, Jargon, and "Insider Speak"

You gain no advantage by confusing your audience. You waste a valuable opportunity to build your brand. Repetition leads to familiarity and familiarity leads to trust.

Step Nine: Do All You Can to Remove Distractions That Can Come Between You and Your Audience

Hiding behind a lectern, reading from notes, or trying to pack too much information into a short time frame are common distractions.

Taking screeds of notes to the lectern shows your audience that you are poorly prepared. Learn to speak from the heart and you will not need notes. If you are not ready to speak without prompters, list your key points on a cue card. There is no shortcut to presenting a powerful presentation. You have to do your homework.

Avoid PowerPoint presentations. For a start, you're asking your audience to split their attention between you and the screen, and, second, you lose the eye contact that will help you read your audience. When I see someone fiddling with a computer before a presentation I shudder inside. Experience tells me I am in for a boring presentation.

Step Ten: If a Microphone Is Available, Use It

Refusing to speak into a microphone is insensitive. There's never a good reason to make your audience strain to hear you. If you are taking questions from someone who is not using a microphone, repeat the question for the whole audience before answering it.

Step Eleven: Always Start Strong with a Powerful Opener

The audience has given you their time, but you have to earn their attention. Making excuses or being self-deprecating, for example, saying, "I'm nervous" or, "I'm not good at speaking in public," is simply a way of telling your audience that you didn't care enough to prepare.

> One of the ways I overcame my fear of speaking was reminding myself that it was not about me, it was about my audience. If you check your ego before you step on stage you will feel more comfortable and come across as more credible.

Step Twelve: If It's Worth Communicating It's Worth Polishing

Asking friends to critique you will help you eliminate habitual mistakes, such as ums and ahs, or overusing certain words or phrases. "Awesome" may be awesome once but repeated ten times it becomes awful.

Practice simple techniques until they become second nature to improve your presentations. Small improvements can make a big difference. For example, using inclusive pronouns, such as *we* and *us*, and talking about "our products, our business, and our team" is a subtle but highly effective way to connect with your audiences.

Step Thirteen: Humor Is Okay, but Be Careful

Humor is a great way to win the attention of your audience, but only if it passes these checks:

- It has to be original. If you recycle other speakers' material, give them credit.

- You must think it's funny. If you don't think it's hilarious, your audience is not going to feel it.

- Don't laugh before your audience does. It can take time to perfect your timing. Practice your punch lines until they're perfect.

- It must be relevant to your audience. A tailored story shows your audience that you're with them and not regurgitating the same material over and over. Everyone loves listening to stories about themselves.

• •

Although I have my favorite openers, I always try to incorporate what I am seeing and feeling at Convention into my presentations. By keeping my eyes and ears open I can almost guarantee I will observe something worth mentioning on stage. Here are two examples:

At many large Conventions the company opens an on-site store for delegates to purchase discounted products and business tools. Network marketers are a competitive lot, and when the store opens there is always a race through the door to nab the best bargains.

When I see this, I open with a solemn, "Before I start my presentation I feel that I should warn you to be careful where you go. There are some very scary places in this city. Last night I walked right into one. Convention Room D. I happened to be standing by the door when they opened the store. I barely escaped with my life." It's funny to the audience because they were there. They created the chaos and they enjoy being teased about it.

Network marketers are also a lively lot, and the atmosphere of Convention is always electric. I rarely have to ask where I am speaking. I just follow the noise.

If Convention is especially lively I may start my presentation by adapting the *What happens in Vegas, stays in Vegas* line with a reminder to my partying audience: "What happens in [Orlando] stays . . ."

I wait until they say, "in Orlando" before I correct them with "on Facebook!" It doesn't matter what city we're in, everyone knows the slogan and it always gets a laugh. What makes it funny is that it's about them.

Always maintain a healthy perspective. If your attempt at humor falls flat, you may feel wounded, but don't let one misstep kill your entire presentation. Don't draw attention to it. We've all heard speakers who admonish the audience for not appreciating their humor. Making your audiences feel bad is not the way to win them over.

The only way to handle a failed attempt at humor is to move on as though you never intended to be funny in the first place. It's better to leave your audience wondering if you fell flat than knowing you did.

Step Fourteen: Adopt a "Two Strikes and It's Out" Rule

If your audience doesn't respond to a point you're making or a story you're sharing, rework it and try again. If they still don't respond, it's time to abandon it. What differentiates a skilled speaker from a so-so communicator is caring enough about your audiences to read the signals they're sending you, and making the necessary improvements. Follow my golden rule of speaking: Make it all about your audience and only about your audience.

Don't be so rigid in your preparation that you don't have a plan B to switch to if your presentation is falling flat. I was at a conference in Europe where the audience was predominantly Russian. I usually find Russian audiences highly responsive, but this time I was either talking too fast or the interpreters were inexperienced (I'll go with the latter) and my opening banter met with a sea of blank faces. I was dying up there until I gave myself this simple pep talk: "Get a grip." I quickly recovered my composure and tried a new angle to win back my audience. Don't prolong your audience's suffering. If it's not working, your audience isn't going to change. You must change.

Step Fifteen: Don't Take Yourself Too Seriously

The most helpful advice I received as I worked on my powers of persuasion was: Your audience is rooting for you. They want you to succeed. The worst advice was to imagine my audience was naked. Whoever came up with that one has clearly never seen my audiences!

The point I am making is, there's nothing to be gained by beating yourself up. Do the best job you can and if it doesn't go over as well as you hoped, try again. It takes practice to become a star performer.

● ● ●

As your business grows, so will your audiences. There's every chance that at some point you'll be on stage as a featured speaker, or accepting an award at your company Convention. The sooner you start using your powerful communication skills, the sooner you'll be ready to step into the spotlight. The more presentations you do, the more competent and confident you'll become.

CHAPTER **13**

Use Print Materials That Reflect Your Best

Few aspects of our business have been reinvented as often as the way we communicate our printed words. Texting and messaging have replaced emailing, we're accessing the bulk of our information on our devices, and we are downloading most of our business brochures.

What hasn't changed is the importance of maintaining professional standards. Nothing shouts "amateur" louder than poorly produced marketing materials.

Your corporate partner spends thousands of dollars producing quality brochures, leaflets, and catalogs. Don't produce your own to save a few dollars, or deface them with sloppy labeling before they reach your customers.

Protect your business and your brand. If you have a good reason to create your own marketing materials (and it has to be really good, when corporate materials can be downloaded or forwarded at minimal expense), make sure you're not diminishing your company's credibility in the process. I would advise not straying from corporate marketing materials. For example, a network marketer received a homemade marketing piece from her sponsor to send on to her customers, and she decided to ask me for feedback.

Although my recommendation was that she not use it, I showed her how to re-sort the information, edit out the errors and repetition, and add her personal story. After I sent my recommendations back, I visited the company website. The branding and messaging were so different that the document could have described another product and another company. It was a clear case of "lost in translation."

Communications created by cutting and pasting from different sources can easily become garbled. I strongly advise that you use your company marketing materials to tell your product story, and focus your efforts on building relationships with your prospects.

You'll always be more effective when your communications are clean, concise, and free of jargon. Get into the habit of editing everything you send out. No matter how many new apps are released, your most powerful communication tool will always be the delete key. If accuracy is not one of your strengths, write your missives offline and do a spelling and grammar check before you send them.

Twitter did the world a huge favor by introducing us to 140 characters. Adapt and adopt the "rule of 140" and you will instantly improve all your communications:

- Condense every text, message, or tweet to a maximum of 140 characters.

- Condense every email or story to a maximum of 140 words.

• •

Incorporate these "less is more" guidelines into your community culture:

- Don't make us scroll down to read your text.

- Don't make us click the "see more" link on your Facebook post.

- If you're convinced that what you're saying needs more than 140 words, break it up with paragraphs or bullet points.

- If you're posting on our team page, think before you post: Is this relevant to the whole team or just adding to the clutter?

Don't take shortcuts when it comes to your products, company name, or titles. Your readers shouldn't have to decipher your jargon, company-speak, abbreviations, or pseudoscientific acronyms.

As we respect our live audiences, we should respect those at the receiving end of our written communications.

> I received an email from a supplier in another country asking if I was interested in sending out an EDM in advance of my next visit. I responded that I wasn't sure, as I didn't know what an EDM was. I did not receive a response.

I'm not suggesting that you avoid creative use of words and phrases. Language is dynamic and evolving. Your customers, hosts, prospects, and team members will respond best when your words reflect your personality. If casual is your natural style, embrace it in all your communications. Your customers, prospects, and team members will appreciate your fresh take on words, phrases, and punctuation. They will enjoy your emoticons.

My speaking style is informal, but when I first started writing I found myself slipping into a more formal style. I solved the problem by visualizing network marketers I knew and writing as though I was speaking to them. When a reader messages me, "When I read your books I hear you speaking to me," I feel that I have succeeded. If it doesn't come naturally, you have to work at it.

With almost one and a half billion of us actively engaging on social media and eight hundred million of us accessing Facebook every day, it makes sense to monitor your online communications to protect your professional image. The next visitor to your page could be a prospective client, host, or team member doing some research before contacting you.

Pause before you unload your personal grievances on a site that potentially the whole world can see. Not only is it unprofessional, it's an open invitation for others to unload their grievances on you.

When you're tempted to let off steam because a neighbor's dog won't stop barking, or the delivery guy dropped your parcel on the driveway, take a few breaths and think, *Who could be reading this? What perception will they have of me? What kind of people do I want to attract to my community?* If you're in any doubt, leave it out!

Stay clear of confrontation. Once your exchanges are in cyberspace, you can neither control nor remove them. There is no delete option once you hit "Send" on your tweet, message, or post.

I post daily tips on Facebook, and because I like to mix things up a little they are sometimes frivolous. After I posted this nonsensical beauty tip to entertain my followers who sell beauty products—*Recommend that your clients get eight hours sleep a night, and nine if they're ugly*—the first comment shot back within seconds. *I'm outraged. That's just rude!* my (former) fan wrote.

A few regulars jumped to my defense, one posting, *I just sent your quote to all my customers with a photo the kids took of me when I got out of bed this morning. They thought it was hilarious!* But a lighthearted post cost me half a day doing damage control. Next time I'll pause before posting a flippant comment on a public page.

However you choose to communicate with your customers, prospects, and team members, make sure what they see in print, on- or off-line, reflects you at your best.

CHAPTER 14

Connect with Audiences by Sharing Your Story

One of the most powerful ways network marketers connect with audiences is by sharing our personal stories. Our stories help us build empathy with our prospects, and start the search for common ground. Mutual interests, experiences, and circumstances are the basis of most relationships.

I almost always share my story during my presentations and in my books. At first it felt uncomfortable, but then I realized that openness was critical to my message, "It doesn't matter where you start in life; it's where you go that counts." I've been thrilled over the years by the number of people who come up to me at conferences, or who later message me to say, "We have a similar story. Knowing that you had a tough start really helps me believe I can achieve what I want to achieve."

Your story is a tool that you can use to inspire your audiences to look beyond their current circumstances and envision what their lives could be. Even though you may be revealing a different life before you started using your products, or started your business, you can't dwell on "the before." Your story should be one of hope and optimism.

If you are still working toward your goals, your story must showcase the progress you have made. You never want people to pity you. You want them to be inspired by you.

Spend time developing your story before you take it to market. You don't get a second chance to make a powerful first impression, and your story must engage your prospects from the start.

Make it brief, so you can quickly turn the attention back to your prospects. We start new relationships by exchanging stories. You can't expect people to be interested in you if you don't show a genuine interest in them.

Your first encounter is not the right time to open the floodgates about your life. You can always flesh out the details another time (if you're asked!).

Your journey is what makes your story interesting. Think about books or movies that captivate you. Whether they're fact, fiction, or fantasy they're always about the journey. You root for your heroes as they overcome their adversities and defeat their adversaries. You jeer when they fail and cheer when they succeed.

Give your audiences more than a sales pitch. Make your journey an integral part of your story. Reveal answers to questions that your audience will find interesting:

- Where did your journey start?
- What prompted you to seek change?
- What challenges did you have?
- How did you overcome them?
- What did you learn?
- How is your life better now?
- What is your next goal?

We relate to people who triumph over challenges because we want to believe we can overcome our own challenges. If you've had to endure someone talking about their achievements without knowing their backstory, you'll know how tedious that can be. Without the journey there is no story. As long as you're not self-pitying, people will empathize with you.

CRAFTING YOUR STORY

A powerful opener will draw your audiences toward you, especially if it tells them what they can expect as your story unfolds. I was drawn into Frank McCourt's book *Angela's Ashes* by two sentences on the memoir's first page: "When I look back on my childhood I wonder how I survived at all. It was of course a miserable childhood; the happy childhood is hardly worth your while." The words promised an interesting story without a trace of self-pity, and all in fewer than 140 characters.

Use your story to inspire, motivate, and build belief in your opportunity. A lackluster story is hardly worth your while.

Curb your urge to get lost in the details. If you are sharing your product story, let your audience know what prompted you to start using the products and what difference they made.

Center your business story on what prompted you to join, what your biggest challenge was, and how your business has enriched your life.

Focus your thoughts by answering these two questions in fifteen seconds or less:

- What inspired you to join?
- What inspires you now?

How did you feel when you answered those questions? Did you feel inspired? If you're not emotionally connected to your own story it's unlikely it will inspire anyone else.

These two simple formats will help you create a story that will have your prospects wanting to know more about you and your business. The stories were shared by network marketers from around the world, and edited by their creators to fit within the "140 word" guideline. Each story demonstrates the power of "less is more" when it comes to making an emotional connection with prospects.

Format One

I first heard about [product/company] when . . .

I decided to join because . . .

The difference it made to my life is . . .

I first heard about [product/company] when a colleague left his job to start a business. At the time I thought he was crazy, although I was envious that he seemed to be having so much fun while I was still stuck at my desk.

I decided to join because he told me how much money he was making. That prompted me to put my prejudices about network marketing aside and listen to what he had to say.

The difference it made to my life is: It was the best decision I ever made. I have a lot to learn but the training and support I've received have been incredible. I'm planning on quitting my job as soon as my business is stable enough. It feels good to know I can take my business full-time when I'm ready.

• • •

I first heard about [product/company] when I was invited to a friend's party. I loved the products so I kept ordering from my distributor's online store.

I decided to join because my distributor called and explained how much I would save if I bought them wholesale. She also showed me how I could make some extra money by selling them to my friends.

The difference it made to my life is: My friends love the products as much as I do. I now have hundreds of customers and I've started building a team. I never thought I would be able to afford to stay home to raise our twins, but my business has made it possible. I love the people I work with, especially the moms who are in a similar situation to me. We support each other.

● ● ●

I first heard about [product/company] when another teacher at school gave out a few samples in the staff room. The products really made a difference so I started using them regularly.

I decided to join because I was burning out at school and had been thinking for a while about trying something different. I've always been interested in nutrition, so the business seemed like a good fit for me.

The difference it made to my life is: The change to our lifestyle has been incredible. I'm using my business earnings to boost our retirement account, and last year I earned a trip to Puerto Vallarta for my wife and me. It was a five-star resort and the company paid for everything. Our lifestyle has completely turned around. I can't wait to quit teaching and do this full-time.

● ● ●

I first heard about [product/company] when a friend talked to me about buying my power from his company. Although my monthly bill was about the same I liked the idea of supporting his small business rather than buying from a big supplier that didn't know I existed.

I decided to join because I could see he was on to something. The company rewards us for signing up new customers, so I started talking to everyone I knew about switching suppliers.

The difference it made to my life is: Everything! I love being my own boss and working to my own schedule. My nine-to-five days are done. The best part is working alongside people who want the same lifestyle as I do. I've even started training to run a marathon, which is something I've wanted to do for ages.

Format Two

Before: . . .

After: . . .

Before: Ever since our first son was born we were never able to pay all our bills each month. We always had to choose which ones to pay. It was costing us hundreds of dollars a month in credit card fees alone. After our daughter arrived I started looking for a way to make some money from home, and that's when I learned about my company.

After: The few hundred dollars a month I bring in has completely changed our financial situation. We're no longer falling behind on our payments, and even our relationship has improved now that some of the stress has been taken off us. I work nights when my husband can babysit. I enjoy getting out of the house for a few hours for some "me" time, and our kids love their exclusive time with dad.

● ● ●

Before: I thought I had the perfect job right up until the day I was made redundant. Apart from the financial stress, I felt so powerless. That's when I vowed I would never put my family in such a vulnerable position again. I coach a local kids' football team, as I have always enjoyed mentoring others, and that's what attracted me to network marketing.

After: I never realized how satisfying it would be. A year after I started, my wife was able to quit her full-time job and join me in the business. We work hard, but we're building our business together and it's been great for our relationship.

● ● ●

Before: It was my high school teacher who first encouraged me to start my own business. As part of our business studies curricu-

lum we had to start and run a profitable business. When our group won the award for "Best Business Venture" our teacher told us, "You'll all be running your own businesses one day."

After: I remembered his words when I went to college. Instead of getting a student loan I sold customized jewelry to pay for my tuition. Everyone loved the jewelry and by the time I graduated my online store was so profitable I decided to work my business full-time. Now I have over three hundred distributors in my organization. Many of them joined during college, and our company Convention always feels like a big college reunion.

• • •

Before: My first sales job was selling kitchen knives door-to-door during college. I stopped when I graduated and began working full-time. Then last year, my former manager contacted me out of the blue to say he had started a business selling insurance and asked if I was interested in working together again. His call came at the perfect time, as our company had just let a few people go and we were all feeling vulnerable. After attending a presentation I applied on the spot, and was accepted into the training program.

After: The company has supported me all the way. The training is incredible and the people I work with are great too. I love helping people, and I feel as though I am doing what I was meant to do.

• • •

Before: I was a shy kid in school so I never expected to end up in sales. But when my uncle offered to help me I decided to give it a try. I was a slow starter, as my biggest challenge was lack of confidence. My uncle suggested that I join Toastmasters to overcome that.

After: Now here I am leading a whole network of salespeople. I can't believe that this is happening to me or that I am helping others overcome their fears to build successful businesses.

• • •

Before: The hardest day of my life was when my husband lost his job and we had to tell our kids they couldn't go to their private school anymore. Although I'd had my network marketing business for a while, I was only playing at it. When I saw the look on my kids' faces I knew what I had to do.

While my husband looked for another job I worked on my business. The more I focused on it, the more profitable it became and that's when we realized how much potential there was to make some serious money.

After: The happiest day of my life was telling my kids they could go back to their school. My husband now has a new job, but we will never put ourselves in such a horrible situation again. My business is here to stay.

• • •

Before: I was a lawyer and I loved my job so much I worked right up until my daughter was born. It was a huge culture shock for me to go from being a full-time lawyer to stay-at-home mom overnight. But my husband and I had always agreed that we wanted our children to have a stay-at-home parent. Then a neighbor invited me to a business presentation and a lightbulb flashed. I could do presentations at night while my husband cared for our daughter.

After: I now have two daughters and a business. I love helping other moms start businesses and it's a lot less stressful than my old job. I will never go back to law now that I have found my dream job.

• • •

Before: I didn't know what I wanted to do with my life, and when I left college my debt was more impressive than my degree. Then about six months ago a guy I met at the gym talked to me about a telecommunications company he had joined. He seemed to be having a great time so I decided to give it a go.

***After:** I'm only twenty-seven, but I have my own business, I'm making money, and I'm having fun. I've learned more about business in the last six months than I learned in three years at college and I'm doing something I enjoy doing. The best part is that my dad has stopped trying to give me advice about how I should live my life. I can tell that he's really proud of me.*

• • •

***Before:** My parents immigrated to the United States when I was four so we've always had close ties to our family in Mexico. But they couldn't afford to visit us, and we could only afford to visit them occasionally. When the company I was working with announced that they were opening in Mexico I was thrilled. I was on a plane to Mexico City within weeks and talking about my business to everyone.*

***After:** More and more people started hearing about it, and my Mexico business exploded. The best part is I can now visit my family anytime I want. Two of my relatives are coming to our company's annual Convention in Orlando this year. Our family has never been closer.*

• • •

***Before:** I wasn't sure about a lot of things when I was twenty-two, but I was sure of one thing: I wasn't going to start my life in debt and living in my parents' basement. I chose network marketing because it was the only way I could start a business without having to borrow money. I'd been saving the tips I earned from my job serving at a local restaurant and I used that to buy myself some time while I learned the ropes.*

***After:** Six months after I started my business I was earning enough to afford to rent an apartment with a friend. My next goal is a car.*

When you have crafted your story, rehearse it to iron out the kinks. Next, video yourself telling it on your computer or phone.

••

When you're recording videos, choose a neutral background, as it will look more professional. Positioning the camera slightly higher than your head and putting a short distance between you and the camera will produce the most flattering angle. If you're recording into a computer, raise its back a little and tilt the screen slightly toward you.

••

After you have recorded your story, play the video back to check that you're coming across as genuine, likable, and enthusiastic. Your presentation doesn't have to be perfect, but you should look for bad habits that distract from your story, such as too many "ums" or "ahs," and work on eliminating them.

If you're not happy with the video, you can delete it and start again. If your story lacks polish, the only solutions are more preparation and more practice.

But don't be overly self-critical, or focus on what you did wrong at the expense of what you did right. You'll never improve by wallowing in your weaknesses. You can always revise and replace your video as you become more accomplished.

When you are happy with your video, post it on your team page and invite your team to record and post their videos too. Next, create a YouTube account and share your story with a broader audience. A YouTube account takes only a few seconds to set up, and with more than a billion users it gives you access to a huge market.

The more places you share your story the more people it will reach.

PART **FOUR**

Leading Your Team

CHAPTER **15**

Techniques for Creating an Engaged Community

Quality of life has always been the driving force of network marketing. We promise a lifestyle that less-adventurous souls can only dream about from their four-by-four cubicles.

One of the greatest advantages of the business is that we work for ourselves, but we're not isolated. Through our network marketing community we can surround ourselves with people who share our aspirations, interests, and values.

Growing a network business is no stroll down easy street. It takes dedication, discipline, and drive to reach a six-figure income, and there will always be those who lack the character to stick with it when the going gets tough. But far too many quit without thinking through their decision, or giving themselves a reasonable chance of succeeding.

You will significantly reduce the dropout rate if you build relationships within your community that go beyond the financial contribution everyone makes. Fulfill their social and emotional needs and they will perform better and stay longer.

I like to think of a network marketing business as operating more like an extended family than a business unit. The closest comparison I can think of comes from my experiences growing up amid the indigenous Maori people of my native New Zealand.

The Maori have a word to describe the notion of extended family. The word is *whanau* (pronounced far-now). Membership of the *whanau* extends to all generations. It includes siblings, aunts, uncles, cousins, and anyone who marries, or is adopted into the *whanau*.

What binds the *whanau* together is kinship.

Historically, *whanau* members shared roles and responsibilities, from producing food and raising children to preserving traditions, values, and culture. Although economic advances eliminated the need for the cooperative responsibilities that once helped the *whanau* manage their daily domestic lives, the spiritual and emotional bonds within the *whanau* have not changed. The *whanau* continues to bond its members together regardless of where they live.

Although America is now my home, I am deeply touched when a Maori refers to me as "auntie." Being given honorary status as a member of the *whanau* makes me feel very special.

Treat everyone within your organization as your extended family. The stronger the bonds your team members have with you and each other, the less likely they are to quit, and the more likely they are to stay around long enough to give their businesses a chance to succeed.

> The reason people join you will not be the reason they stay. They will stay when they are among people who make them feel included, liked, and appreciated.

Include your team's family members in your community. More often than not, our families are involved in our businesses. Some spouses work alongside us as equal partners, while others support us by delivering orders, taking calls, or managing the books. Our children help us pack our demonstration kits and unpack our orders. We don't see the need to keep our business and family lives separate. By making family members feel welcome, included, and appreciated, you reinforce that you're a family business.

It's more than taking care of business. By nurturing your relationships with your team members and encouraging them to build relationships with each other, the more fulfilling everyone's experience will be.

Many charismatic leaders build their network marketing businesses quickly. Charisma is a magnet but it's not powerful enough to hold a business long term. The leader who genuinely cares about every team member's well-being will always have more sustainable success.

I've been fortunate to work alongside many of this industry's highest income earners across a range of companies. What makes them exceptional does not come from flashy displays of affection or appreciation. It's the small gestures that demonstrate their genuine empathy for their people. If you fake it, no one's going to feel it.

I was attending a leadership retreat organized by a top field leader. As the retreat ended she asked, "Does everyone have a ride to the airport?" It was hard to hear her over the noise of people packing up to leave but she persisted. "I want to make sure everyone has a ride." She looked out over the room. "Cindy, do you have your ride organized? Carol, who are you going with?" As she spoke I could see her eyes going from table to table checking that everyone was taken care of. She wasn't micromanaging. She was taking care of her people. When you take care of your people, they will take care of your business.

Start the process of making every team member feel special the day he or she joins. Welcome new members by posting their photo and an introduction on your Facebook group page. You can almost guarantee the welcome messages from other team members will start flowing immediately. There is a big difference between explaining that they have the support of a whole community and creating an opportunity for them to experience it.

PAYING ATTENTION TO THE SMALL DETAILS

Ease new team members' assimilation into the community. Introduce them at the start of every meeting until you can see that they're confidently interacting with other team members. Make the wearing of name badges mandatory at all events to help new team members learn names. The sooner they work out who's who, the sooner they will feel part of the team. Introduce new team members to each other at meetings, as you would introduce guests with similar interests and circumstances to each other at a party in your home.

Prepare an electronic cue card for all new people when they join, noting basic family details such as other jobs they have, their partner's name and job, the names and ages of their children, and their personal interests outside the business. You don't have to become immersed in their lives to show you care, but there's a big difference between asking, "How's your husband's new job working out?" and, "How's Geoff enjoying his new job at Delta?"

ADDRESSING ANY CONCERNS
NEW PEOPLE MAY HAVE UP FRONT

For example, you want them to come to Convention and experience the excitement of being part of the corporate community as soon as possible.

But as an empathetic leader, you know they may feel uncertain about what to expect at Convention. Traveling alone or leaving family behind can be a big deal for first timers. The sheer size of Convention may be overwhelming, and newcomers won't know details that experienced Convention goers take for granted. "What should I wear?" is a good example. You don't want them finding reasons not to come because they're worrying about small details.

ANTICIPATING AND ADDRESSING THEIR CONCERNS BEFORE THEY BECOME AN ISSUE

Stay close to new team members for the first three months. Relationships take time to develop, and the more contact new members have with you throughout that period the stronger your bonds will become. Relationships are like all living organisms. They thrive in environments where there is a constant supply of nurturing and nourishment.

CONNECTING WITH INDIVIDUAL TEAM MEMBERS

Incorporate strategies that will strengthen your bonds with team members into your business plan:

- Send cards on their birthdays and anniversary-of-joining dates.
- Keep yourself updated with what's happening in their personal lives.
- Show your support during personal or family crises.
- Schedule weekly one-on-one phone calls with your most productive team members.
- Engage your smaller performers on Facebook, and encourage them to come to meetings.
- Pay attention. When you see an increase, decrease, or change in results, get in touch. If a team member who has been performing consistently suddenly stops placing orders, you know something has changed. A timely phone call may lead to a valuable conversation about the business. At the very least it will show your team members that you care.

- Keep your antenna on high alert so you don't miss the signals they're sending. The timing of support and encouragement can make a huge difference. Many times I have picked up a clue from someone on Facebook, sent a supportive message, and received a message back saying, "I needed to hear that today," or, "Your message came at the right time."

- Schedule monthly team meetings. If it's not geographically realistic for everyone to gather together, virtual meetings can be equally productive. If you have a sizable group who can get together in one place, set up a webcam for those who can't make the live meeting.

- Spend a few minutes chatting one-on-one with team members before or after meetings, especially those who do not get weekly calls. No one wants to feel excluded or invisible.

- Applaud achievements and address concerns immediately. Delaying recognition or not responding quickly when team members reach out to you is a sign of insincerity.

- Be consistent. A disorganized or erratic approach to maintaining relationships is not the way to build loyalty, trust, and confidence in your leadership.

- Invite your leaders and their partners to your home, a game, or a restaurant for a social dinner.

- Make frequent thoughtful, spontaneous gestures. For example, "I found these stands for my holiday display and got one for you too," or "I just read a brilliant book on team building. Would you like to borrow it?"

- Be willing to travel at least once a year to meet face-to-face with your geographically remote team members. If that's not possible, do all you can to get them to Convention, and give them extra time and attention when they do attend.

CONNECTING YOUR TEAM MEMBERS WITH EACH OTHER

The benefit of building a close community is that everyone becomes a stakeholder and will support each other. Bolster that feeling of community by:

- Encouraging them to share their goals, achievements, and stories.

- Recognizing birthdays, personal milestones, and achievements in your team communications.

- Choosing a local charity or cause to support as a team. It doesn't have to involve fund-raising. Many local charities will appreciate you volunteering your time.

- Inviting team members to work vendor events together.

- Inviting them to interact on Facebook, and support each other with information, feedback, or advice.

CONNECTING AT MEETINGS

All live events, from your team meetings to your corporate Conventions, create the perfect opportunity to strengthen the bonds within your team. They'll be more likely to attend if you give them a reason to participate beyond training. Always make fun and fellowship an integral part of events.

More team members will come to meetings if you:

- Create an energizing, celebratory environment with music, signage, and staging.

- Create fun themes, such as *Go Green* for St. Patrick's Day, *We LOVE Our Team* for Valentine's Day, and the destination of your annual incentive trip at the start of qualification.

- Schedule a five-minute "shout-out" session at team meetings for sharing personal and/or business news.

- Play relationship-building games at meetings (see suggested games below).

- Encourage interaction, brainstorming, and idea sharing at every meeting.

- Award fun trophies to those who contribute beyond business performance. For example: *Always First to Arrive*, *Travels the Farthest Distance*, *Brightest Light*, and *Team Spirit* awards.

- Create opportunities for everyone to be a VIP. For example, reserve front-row seating for team members who bring a guest, or are celebrating birthdays, date-of-joining anniversaries, or special achievements.

- Replace regular team meetings with two to three social events a year, such as a midsummer family barbecue at a local park, a midwinter holiday party, or a team bowling tournament.

- Create and award "cash vouchers" for meeting attendance, achievements, or participation in any role from presenting to registration to arranging the music. Vouchers can be saved up and spent at a lively auction of products, business tools, and gifts at the first meeting of the following year (guaranteed to lead to a big turnout to kick-start the new year).

- Give value. Always incorporate information, inspiration, or ideas they can take home from the meeting to make their attendance worthwhile.

Involve your team in meetings by delegating tasks such as display, signage, music, or refreshments, but never delegate the "meet and greet." Be at the door when team members arrive and as they leave. If you're setting up your display, or are deep in conversation with one person while others stand alone, you have wasted an opportunity to make many people feel important.

Relationship-Building Games for Team Meetings

SPEED NETWORKING!

Circulate a *Who Am I?* quiz with personal and business clues about individual team members. Challenge everyone to find the person who matches each description. For example:

- *Who has three children?*
- *Who has been married the longest time?*
- *Who's engaged to be married?*
- *Who has a birthday this month?*
- *Who loves chocolate?*
- *Who joined in the last six months?*
- *Who recently sponsored their first team member?*
- *Who has sales exceeding a thousand dollars this month?*
- *Who won an award at last year's Convention?*

Praise those who complete the card for their superb networking skills.

TEAM BINGO!

Prepare a nine-square bingo card with descriptions that fit one or more team members and ask everyone to find someone who matches the description. For example:

- *Has four appointments scheduled this week*
- *Has already registered for Convention*
- *Was born in 1995*
- *Has the same birth month as you*
- *Earned the incentive trip for two*
- *Promoted to a higher rank this year*
- *Is celebrating her joining anniversary this month*
- *Signed two new recruits this month*
- *Has two children*
- *Is a flight attendant*
- *Joined in the last two months*

Reward everyone who completes the card with small prizes.

FUN FACTS!

Circulate fun questions to team members at random, and ask them to share their answers. For example:

- *What is your most irrational fear?*
- *What is your favorite food?*
- *What is your least favorite food?*
- *What was your greatest childhood talent?*
- *Tell us something that no one here knows about you!*
- *What is your dream car?*
- *Who is your secret movie-star crush?*
- *What do you dream about?*
- *If you won an open-destination plane ticket where would you go?*

FUN FACTS VERSION TWO!

This variation is similar to the game above but each team member thinks up a question and writes it on a slip of paper. Everyone then draws a question at random to answer.

FACT OR FICTION!

Each team member takes turns to share an experience he or she has had. Everyone then votes on whether the shared experience is fact or fiction.

WHO AM I?

Each team member writes a fact about himself or herself on paper. Gather up the papers, draw them out at random, and read them out. Everyone tries to match the fact to its owner.

FAST FINGERS!

Circulate a sheet of craft paper to all team members and give them three minutes to create an origami "masterpiece." Everyone votes on whose masterpiece is the best!

FLYING FINGERS!

Circulate a sheet of craft paper to all team members and give them three minutes to create a paper plane. Invite them to line up in small groups and fly their plane. The person whose plane travels the farthest wins each heat. Winners of each heat compete for the glory of supreme winner.

• •

CONNECTING WITH CORPORATE

Team members who are plugged into the company tend to produce more and stay longer. Nowhere is this more evident than with those who attend Convention.

Promote Convention as a highlight of the calendar and something the team does together. As attending Convention can run to several hundred dollars, it pays to promote Convention throughout the year to give team members time to budget the time and expense involved.

- Talk often about the value that Convention offers.

- Promote a variety of benefits (networking, celebrating, free gifts, breaking news, fun, new products, social events, gaining new ideas at workshops, inspirational speakers) to appeal to different motivations.

- Encourage everyone to take advantage of early-bird registration.

- Share travel tips, for example, cheap airfare or accommodation deals.

- Organize team costumes. They can be as simple as a team T-shirt or something more elaborate if your team enjoys dressing up, or your company includes a theme party as part of its Convention.

- Share "what to expect" and "not-to-be-missed" highlights.

- Fuel the fire with a flow of lively messages:
  - When you show up, you go up! The environment of friendship and fun at Convention is the perfect place to gain the inspiration and ideas you need to take your business to the next level.
  - Convention is a highlight of our year.
  - Convention is when we take a break from our businesses to refresh, recharge, and re-energize ourselves.

Once you have arrived at Convention make your team members' experience your top priority.

- Check that everyone has someone to room with and that team members with conflicting lifestyles are not rooming together (e.g., party-all-nighters with early-to-risers!).

- Host an arrival night reception in your room or the hotel restaurant. Don't be too ambitious or stray too far from the hotel the first night, as people may be delayed or arrive exhausted. You don't want their Convention experience to start with disappointment.

- Be readily available throughout Convention. Emotions can run high at Convention, and the sooner you deal with drama the better.

- Keep the team connected. If the program permits, organize a few team get-togethers during Convention, such as team breakfasts, a team dinner, a pre-gala dinner social hour/photo opportunity, or an excursion on free nights (in-room pizza delivery is fine if your budget is tight!).

Never be too busy to nurture your relationships. I've seen whole companies crumble when the bonds between owners and sales force are weakened. Showing an interest in your team members beyond the contribution they make to your bottom line will always pay dividends.

VALUING YOUR TEAM MEMBERS

A leader appreciates every person's contribution, big or small, and through the upturns and downswings alike. Anyone can manage relationships when things are going well, but a true leader always puts people over profits:

- Take nothing for granted and no one for granted. Even the smallest upset can destabilize a business. It only takes one person to fall out of the boat for it to start capsizing!

- Don't let success go to your head. Swollen egos are the root cause of many shrinking businesses.

- Value diversity. Make it a priority to nurture relationships with all team members without being distracted by personal preferences or prejudices.

- Set high expectations when it comes to harmony within your organization. Your business is certain to include a range of personalities, and they won't all click naturally. Don't let personality clashes undermine team spirit.

- Always share the credit when you are promoted or recognized for a team achievement. Use the achievement to bolster team spirit and morale.

Don't Abandon Relationships When People Leave
No leader likes to lose a team member, but you must be gracious and supportive when it happens. It's inevitable that you will lose team members, and how you handle their departure will speak volumes about your leadership. By leaving the door open and welcome mat out you'll make it easy for them to return as customers, hosts, or even team members. Here's an example of what to say:

We're going to miss you. But I'm glad we had the opportunity to work together and I appreciate the contribution you made. I know you'll be a huge success whatever you choose to do next. Let's stay in touch. I'll keep sending you catalogs, and I'll invite you to any VIP events we hold. If you and your friends need anything, you can order it through me and I'll take care of you.

Thought-starters for aspiring leaders:

- Am I investing enough time in my relationships?
- Do I know enough about my team members?
- How will I get to know them better?
- How will I welcome new people onto my team?
- How will I make prospects and guests feel welcome but not overwhelmed?
- How will I strengthen bonds with my team members?
- How will I build my team members' bonds with each other?
- How will I create harmony within my team?
- How will I make my smaller players feel valued and important?
- How will I support my high performers?
- How will I encourage everyone to attend Convention?
- How will I add more fun and fellowship to my meetings?
- How will we handle disagreements?
- What steps could I implement to strengthen our relationships?

Putting People Before Profits
Jessica Kim, president, Barefoot Books

As we run our businesses it's tempting to focus on our results. But in the midst of going after our end goals, we can easily miss the true heart of what makes this business really work.

We are a relationship-based business. When you step back and think about the relationships in your life, the most powerful ones are built over multiple experiences. Meeting someone at a friend's party can be enjoyable, but it takes time and several interactions before trust starts to build.

Gradually our positive first impressions turn into a solid understanding of that person. The walls come down and our conversations become more open. We start caring about the person and about his or her needs. We want to be supportive and help the person find solutions to any problems because we *genuinely care*.

In network marketing we're not just selling products. We're creating customized solutions for our customers. Customized doesn't mean the product is unique, or that it was specifically made for one customer. Customized means that we genuinely care about our customer's needs and how our products will meet them.

When I receive a marketing email from most companies, I know that I am one of a million people who received that email, and I disregard it. When people I know reach out to me with offers and suggestions, I take the time to listen to what they're saying because I know that they understand my needs.

People know when they are being sold to. No one wants that. Our most successful ambassadors are those who genuinely care about their customers' needs rather than how they will benefit from making the sale.

Build your business by nurturing authentic relationships. Make time to get to know your customers and to engage with them frequently. Take an interest in what's happening in their lives and let them know it. Comment on their Facebook posts, ask questions, and listen to their answers. Look at them as people, and not just as potential customers or team members.

If you approach your relationships with genuine care, you'll create a loyal community of followers. Business will come *to you* rather than you having to seek it out.

The same approach works for leaders. The most successful leaders in our business see their team as their bloodlines. They put themselves in their team members' shoes and proactively provide what they need. They genuinely care about their team members over and above their sales. They take time to find out why they joined, what their goals are, and where their roadblocks are.

When you genuinely care about your customers, the sales will follow. When you genuinely care about your team members they will be more loyal and more dedicated.

Many network marketers are attracted to a company because of its products, but products alone aren't enough to grow a sustainable business. The strength of your business will depend on how much time you invest in your people and how much you genuinely care about their needs.

CHAPTER 16

Get the Benefits of Coaching Without Sapping Your Time

Coaching will always be one of the most satisfying aspects of your business. Nothing compares to the thrill you feel when a team member you mentor rises up the ranks.

Coaching can also be a major drain on your time. The following guidelines will help you provide the environment and opportunity for your team members to flourish without becoming overwhelmed or dropping the ball on other commitments.

DON'T CONFUSE THE ROLES OF COACH AND TRAINER

Coaches focus on action, not information. They guide, support, and encourage their team members to cultivate the strengths that will help them advance and eliminate the weaknesses that pose a threat to their progress.

Many aspiring leaders fall into the training trap because it's comfortable for them. But training on basic information that your team members can access themselves is a terrible waste of your time.

More information does not lead to more action. Experience is the best teacher, and your team members will learn their most valuable lessons at the front lines, making calls, consulting, and presenting. That's when they will benefit most from your guidance, encouragement, and support.

Success in network marketing cannot be achieved by making one bold move. It can only be achieved by taking a series of small steps. Focus on the steps your team members need to take at each stage of their progress. When you know what they need to do, you'll know what they need to know.

INVEST THE BULK OF YOUR TIME IN TEAM MEMBERS WHO ARE WILLING TO WORK

You'll always have team members who demand more time and more training. Not only will it be exhausting for you, it's unlikely to lead to results. Sooner or later they will have to take the field. You'll be cheering them on, but you won't be running the ball with them.

Approach coaching the way you would approach a game of tennis. Once you hit the ball into their court, the next move is theirs to make. There's no value in lobbing another ball over the net before they've returned the first one.

Every team member will grow at his or her own pace. You can't force it, and trying to coax a person to perform above his or her current skill level can be counterproductive. Imagine how your third-grader would feel if he suddenly found himself in a class of fifth-graders.

DON'T BE IN A RUSH TO PROVIDE ANSWERS

Your team members won't learn to independently research information or solve their own problems if you do it for them. Learn to ask:

- "Where have you looked?"
- "What have you tried?"
- "What do you think?"

SET AN EXPECTATION OF
INDEPENDENCE FROM THE START

New team members will always need extra guidance, but don't encourage them to make you their go-to for basic information. Purposefully guide them toward becoming independent as soon as possible by showing them where to find the answers they're seeking.

- "That's a good question. It's covered on page eight in your distributor guide."
- "The best place to find that answer is the policy guidelines you received in your Starter Kit."
- "If you go to your business center and click on 'Events' it's all there."
- "There is an excellent webinar on handling objections under 'Training Resources' in your workstation. I found it very helpful. Call me after you've listened to it. I'd love to know if it helps you."

DON'T ASSUME YOUR TEAM MEMBERS
ARE ABSORBING INFORMATION

Listening is the least effective way to learn. Avoid key information falling on deaf ears by encouraging feedback. With a little preparation you can turn important information into interactive exercises that slot smoothly into meetings, calls, or webinars.

EXERCISE #1

Objective is to help everyone understand exactly how to qualify for the annual incentive trip.

At the start of the qualifying period, ask everyone to bring the Incentive Trip Qualifying Guidelines to the meeting. Asking them to bring their own notes will reinforce your message of personal responsibility.

Ask a question and recognize the first person to find the correct answer:

- *What is the maximum number of credits we can earn for personal sales?*

- *How many credits do we earn for sponsoring?*

- *What is the cumulative value of orders our new recruits must place before we can earn the sponsoring credits?*

- *What is the deadline for placing those orders?*

- *Are the qualification figures wholesale or retail?*

- *How many credits do we earn by promoting to director?*

- *What is the quickest way to accumulate credits?*

EXERCISE #2

Objective is to avoid disappointment by coaching team members not to take it to the wire when aiming for incentives. A scramble to rally your stragglers at the eleventh hour is not leadership.

Using the Incentive Guidelines, ask questions that will minimize team members' risk of missing out on the reward because of poor planning or procrastination:

- *What date does the incentive start?*

- *What steps could you take now to give yourself a flying start?*

– *What date does the incentive end?*

– *What cutoff date should you aim for?*

– *What months are most likely to produce our best sales?*

– *What months could potentially be our slowest?*

– *What steps can we take to increase sales in those months?*

EXERCISE #3

Objective is to maximize the potential of a new catalog.

Ask everyone to bring a catalog and find answers to these questions:

– *Which sets offer the best value?*

– *Which products are likely to be most popular?*

– *Are there any limited-edition offers that may run out early?*

– *What makes them stand out?*

– *How many items do we have under $20 [$30]?*

– *What product or offer creates the best add-on or up-sell opportunity at checkout?*

– *Where are the hidden gems in the catalog?*

– *Which products will you personally be highlighting?*

– *Why is it best to book appointments as early as possible?*

EXERCISE #4

Objective is to improve team members' selling skills.

Invite experienced team members to randomly draw the name of a product and "sell" the benefits of the product or offer to the group.

EXERCISE #5

Objective is to ensure that team members understand the difference between features and benefits.

This simple variation on Exercise #4 will help reinforce the difference between features and benefits. Although this is a simple concept to understand it's not as easy to do. A little rehearsal in a lively atmosphere will help team members learn to avoid lapsing into selling features during their live performance.

When each team member takes a turn to "sell" a product, the rest vote on whether each point made illustrated a feature or a benefit. You will add to the fun if you hand each person two colored cards (with one color representing features and the other benefits) to hold up instead of voting verbally.

EXERCISE #6

Objective is to highlight the requirements and rewards of promoting to the next level of leadership.

Form a panel of team members who have already earned the leadership title. Invite them to take turns to talk about an additional benefit they receive at that level. Include privileges such as an invitation to the leadership conference, or participation in leadership calls, rather than focusing solely on the financial benefits.

After the presentations encourage the audience to ask questions of the panelists.

• •

Quick coaching tip: When you are coaching on the compensation plan always convert percentages into dollars. It's hard to get anyone excited by percentages. You can't spend a percentage.

• •

ELIMINATE OUTDATED, SUPERFLUOUS, OR REPETITIOUS TRAINING MATERIALS

We're drowning in information! Don't add to the clutter. Find ways to reduce the volume of information your team members receive.

This especially applies to blindly passing on materials. No one is going to be inspired by a bunch of recycled handouts. If they're worth sharing, they're worth polishing. A few simple edits will go a long way toward making information more appealing.

The same applies to sharing images. If they're worth sharing, they're worth reducing or expanding to the correct size. If the original image is imperfect, don't share it.

Your team members will take their lead from you, and by taking a lackadaisical approach to sharing materials you are communicating that it's acceptable to "make do" or cut corners. Good enough is only good enough when your standards are high enough.

I was speaking at the leader retreat, where the back table overflowed with handouts from previous retreats. The typefaces were different, some had been altered by hand, and some copied so often they were faded and off-center. As I was waiting for my turn to speak I gathered them up and amid the clutter found a gem of an idea, which I shared during my presentation.

"Wait!" said a number of my audience members in unison. "That's brilliant. Can you repeat what you just said so we can write it down?"

"You already have it," I said. "I found it in your handouts."

Then I asked, "Who's already taken a set of those handouts?" All hands went up.

"Who will actually read those handouts?" Most hands started wavering.

"Who will probably take them home and file them away until your next big cleanout when you'll toss them?" After a thoughtful pause, most hands went up again.

I have no doubt that the leader's intention was to give her team as much information as possible. But it was misguided. Had she asked someone to summarize the information, she would have produced at most one page of "best ideas." Throwing information about and hoping some of it will stick is neither effective communication nor leadership.

KEEP THEM INSPIRED WITH A CONSTANT FLOW OF IDEAS

The key to coaching is a little, often. Always be on the lookout for fresh ideas to share with your team members. In my book *Be a Party Plan Superstar* I use the word *sparks* to describe simple tips, techniques, or tricks that will keep your team inspired, encouraged, and excited.

Break key training topics into manageable sections. Two twenty-minute segments are enough training for any meeting, and one ten-minute segment enough for any weekly call.

A variety of presenters will always make information more interesting. Delegate different topics to team members. This gives your guest presenters an opportunity to improve their communication skills while they are making a contribution.

Gather ideas and information from books, videos, and meetings, and share, share, share. Every time you share an idea it gains in value. The more people who act on it, the more valuable it becomes. Above all, don't hold on to information. Good ideas don't get better if you cellar them. They become old and moldy.

Put your phone to work at corporate meetings and Convention. Message breaking news and fresh ideas to your team members on a Convention newsfeed.

WORK SMART

Embrace the wealth of training resources your company provides and spend your time coaching new people and performers.

If your corporation or sponsor leans a little heavily on information, summarize it into "All you need to know" fact sheets.

Customers don't buy, hosts don't book, and prospects don't join because they're informed. They buy, book, and join because they're inspired. Real-life examples, demonstrations, and experiences will always pack more punch than facts and statistics.

If they can't see it, feel it, or experience it,
you face an uphill battle getting them to buy it.

COACH YOUR PEOPLE TO PROVIDE SOLUTIONS

One of the most valuable lessons your team members will learn is that you have to identify problems before you can credibly offer solutions. Hammer this message home at every opportunity: Your customers and prospects know what they want. Your job is to find out what they want.

I am sure you've had many similar experiences to this one. Wandering past a bag store I saw a display of men's wallets that reminded me that my husband needed a new one. I had barely entered the store when a sales assistant leapt out and said, "Are you looking for a bag? These ones just came in." Before I could respond she picked up the closest handbag and asked, "Do you like these?" The pressure was too much and I lost my appetite for shopping. As I exited the store, she made one last attempt to bag me. "Everything on this side of the store is on special today."

I wish the same thing never happened in our business but it does. I get daily Facebook or LinkedIn messages from people who haven't bothered to look at my profile: "Have you heard of [company]? We're looking for business partners like you," or, "I am excited about an opportunity I have discovered. Please click this link and let me know what you think."

It's so clumsy I wonder how it ever works. Don't let it happen in your organization. Whether they are attempting to sell products or the business opportunity, coach your team members to ask questions and listen to the answers *before* they start offering solutions.

BE A BUSINESS COACH, NOT A LIFE COACH

You're a coach, not a counselor. Care about your team members but don't get swallowed up by their personal issues, or situations that are not business related. You'll quickly burn out if you try to be all things to all team members.

Protect your team members from personal drama by consistently communicating "Let's keep it positive" messages throughout the team.

When team members post something inappropriate or overly personal on your team page, contact them privately and ask them to stop. Gently remind them that everyone has issues to deal with. The whole team will be dragged down if every team member uses your page as a complaints bulletin, or therapy session. That's what family and friends were invented for.

Even the slightest hint of negativity can be highly contagious. As I was writing this book, I posted two requests one week apart on my Facebook page:

The first was, share your pet Facebook peeve. The second was, share one thing your sponsor or team leader did that made you feel special.

In twenty-four hours I received over 150 responses to the first question and only 12 responses to the second. The disparity was so glaring it was a sharp reminder to stay on the sunny side of the street.

DON'T BE A PUSHOVER

One of your greatest challenges will come from demands by team members who are a little lazy. Spoiler alert: They're usually the ones who don't show up to team meetings or webinars. Set boundaries. Your time is precious and you need to spend it on your performers.

This is a sensitive issue for many leaders, but if you don't place a high value on your time, no one else will. Put steps in place to manage excessively demanding team members:

- Set "office hours" when you respond to individual emails and messages. Circulate those times to the team, saying, "This is the best time to reach me, and when I respond to personal messages."

- Unless it is a private issue, encourage your team members to post their questions on Facebook, where everyone can benefit from the answer. An added benefit of this approach is that other team members will often jump in with an answer before you have time to address them.

- When someone contacts you privately, say: "Why don't you ask other team members for their input? I would like to hear their suggestions too."

- If one team member appears to be asking too many questions, say: "I love how eager you are to learn. You would gain so much by coming to training."

- If someone messages you too often, slow the conversation down by delaying your responses.

When you accept empty promises and excuses over performance you're teaching your weaker team members to dump their problems on you.

MAKE PERSONAL ACTIVITY
YOUR TOP PRIORITY

Never lose sight of the fact that personal activity is the only aspect of your business you can truly control. Don't become so involved in helping your team that you neglect the most important aspect of your business, personal activity!

CHAPTER 17

How to Guide Your Vulnerable Rookies

The most magical moment in every distributor's career is the day he or she starts a business. At this point anything and everything is possible. Some of them will achieve success beyond their wildest dreams.

The luckiest ones will have the support of a committed, caring sponsor who has walked in their shoes, a sponsor who has traveled the path they're on and who is willing to guide them.

The greatest gift you can give new team members is your support when they need it most. As they start their journey they have lots to learn in a short amount of time. You know that the path won't be smoothly paved, and how a few bumpy patches can quickly dent their belief. You also know how easy it is for a new distributor to make the wrong moves or veer off track. The last thing you want is to lose new recruits before they've had every chance of success.

Remember that the statistics are not on their side. Half of all distributors abandon their businesses in the first three months. But here's the heartening news. My experiences tell me that the number one cause of failure for new distributors is inexperienced leadership.

This is where you can make a difference. Your experienced, empathetic guidance will give your new team members the support and encouragement they need to survive the first three months, and thrive for years to come.

Excitement and enthusiasm are not enough to successfully launch a business. Success goes to those who take the right steps at the right time to set themselves up for success beyond their first few months.

Use your knowledge and experiences during this "make-or-break" time to help new recruits through the most vulnerable stage of their businesses:

- Get them started as soon as possible.

- Make their journey as rewarding as possible.

- Smooth out as many bumps in the road as possible.

I have heard countless successful distributors share stories of how they would have quit without the support of a sponsor who encouraged them when the going got rough, or believed in them when their confidence waivered.

Flash back to the day you started your business. What if you knew then what you know now? What if you'd had a mentor to guide you through your first steps? Someone who knew exactly what you had to do and when to do it, who knew where you could fall and how to recover if you did.

Invest as much time as possible in new recruits during their first three months. Don't try to second-guess them, or jump to judgment about who has the makings of a performer or a plodder. Not all winners are fast out of the gate. Everyone paces himself or herself differently. It takes at least three months to produce an accurate picture of recruits' potential, and the support they'll need during the next phase of their business.

Potential leadership indicators at the three-month mark:

- Warm personality
- Optimistic attitude
- Consistent activity
- Has started to recruit
- Regularly servicing customers
- Wants to increase income
- Willing to commit the time

Plan and implement a duplicable start-up program for all new recruits. Share it with everyone in your organization so they can follow your lead. Duplicable programs are the only way to give every new recruit an equal shot at success.

Blend your company's training and reward programs for new distributors with these steps to give your recruits the support they deserve.

STEP ONE: SET THEIR COMPASS

Launching a business is like launching a rocket ship. No matter how powerful its thrust, it must be pointed in the right direction.

One of the greatest threats all home-based entrepreneurs face is distraction. Although it's impossible to eliminate all distractions, you can help minimize them by making sure your new recruits know exactly where they're going. If they're vague about their goal they could easily lose direction.

Don't complicate it. Explain that it's as simple as deciding where they want to be and going there. Focus their thinking with questions:

- What does success mean to you?
- If you earned $20,000 from your business this year what would you spend it on?

- What if you earned $50,000?

- What difference would an extra $500 a week make to your life?

- If you could make one personal wish come true this year what would it be?

- If you could make one family dream come true this year what would it be?

The more passionate they are about their goal, the more focused they will be, and the lower the threat of distraction will be. Helping new team members identify a goal with enough firepower to maintain thrust takes leadership.

You need empathy and patience to uncover a true goal as compared to a hastily conceived goal, or the "sensible" goal they think they should have. We are driven by what we want, not what we need.

Asking a quick-fire question may help: "You just won $10,000. What are you spending it on?" Spontaneous answers often produce the most accurate reflection of our innermost motivations.

Don't take it too far or move too fast. It's too soon to be talking about a six-figure income or sailing away on a luxury cruise ship (unless your company just announced a cruise as its incentive trip). Keep the focus close. Grandiose goals with blurry timelines are not going to create the urgency new recruits need to start working now. Focus them on one goal, one year, one step at a time.

STEP TWO: BOLSTER THEIR BELIEF IN THE BUSINESS AND THEMSELVES

It takes only a few small setbacks for confidence to start draining away. Empathetic leaders know how important it is to keep replenishing their community's belief in the business and themselves.

This is especially critical for new recruits when they have so much to learn. Start them strong by affirming your confidence in them. For example: "I know you can do it and I'm looking forward to helping you. What's important now is that you don't let anything distract you from reaching your goal. A few setbacks are normal, and if you have any problems we'll work together to find a way around them. As long as you are willing to work, and willing to learn, I have no doubt that you'll succeed."

We don't abandon our car when we have a minor collision or malfunction. We fix the problem, so that we can get back on the road and on to our destination. Take the same approach to your business. The sooner you identify and fix a problem, the sooner you will be back on track to achieve your goal.

Reaffirm your confidence in them often. When they encounter obstacles, remind them: "This is a temporary setback. As long as you stay focused on your goal and don't let yourself get thrown off track by the highs and lows you'll get there. Learning to take setbacks in stride is part of the learning process we all go through."

STEP THREE: ASK FOR THEIR COMMITMENT

One of your greatest risks is that your new recruits will underestimate the potential of their new business. They wouldn't walk away if they invested $200,000 to $300,000 in a franchise, but here they've invested only a few hundred dollars. This is why you need to emphasize the value of the business, and not what they invested to start it.

Sharing your first experiences will help build empathy and trust. For example:

When I started my business I had no idea that I could make such a success of it. I joined because [we had some hefty medical bills to pay]. Since then everything has changed. In the first year we were able to [pay off our debt and start saving for our own home]. I no longer think about going back to a regular job. I'm already earning what I used to earn working full-time and I get to stay home with my wife and kids. I never dreamed this could happen to me, and I know it can happen for you too.

Now it's time to ask for their commitment:

I've already promised to do everything I can do to help you. But I want you to promise me two things. First, that you won't underestimate the potential of your new business because of the small financial investment you've made. You have my support, and the support of a whole company behind you. You can take your business anywhere you want it to go.

The second promise is that you won't give up until you achieve what you set out to achieve. It's your business, and you'll decide how much time and effort you're willing to put into it, but I want to know that you're as committed to achieving your goal as I am to helping you.

By setting an expectation of commitment you start your business relationship on the right track.

STEP FOUR: REDUCE THEIR PAPERWORK SO THEY'LL HAVE MORE TIME FOR PEOPLE WORK

You'll save rookies a lot of time and uncertainty if you download a calendar covering their first three months, and mark it up with their key dates:

- Deadlines for their new distributor rewards
- New distributor training
- Team meetings
- Company events
- Current company incentives

- Business launch
- Observation meeting (where they accompany you to one of your appointments)

Their own website can be a big distraction. And you can help them avoid wasting hours on the corporate website by pointing to key areas they should visit first.

Absorbing masses of product knowledge can also be a big time stealer. Suggest that they start with a few core products or services for their first appointments and gradually add more as they gain confidence.

Making sure they know what their best first steps are will also help prevent them from spending time in unproductive areas. Taking these initial steps should be their top priority:

- Creating their contacts list
- Inviting guests to their business launch event
- Making appointments and bookings
- Sharing their products and/or services

STEP FIVE: ATTEND THEIR BUSINESS LAUNCH TO MEET THEIR INNER CIRCLE OF CONTACTS

The business launch gives you the perfect opportunity to identify your rookies' first recruit among their inner circle. This is an all-win situation:

- They will earn the new distributor sponsoring reward.
- They will be one person toward becoming a leader.
- You will have replaced your new recruit if he or she leaves.
- You are giving a new person an opportunity to start a business.

Every guest who attends the business launch will increase your rookies' chances of getting their first appointments and recruits. Suggest they schedule it as soon as possible, invite as many guests as they can, and call guests personally before sending out the invitations. They will lessen the risk of no-shows by calling to remind their guests two days before the launch.

STEP SIX: SCHEDULE APPOINTMENTS AND BOOKINGS

The sooner new distributors learn how to generate appointments and bookings the better. Make it clear that their first appointments and bookings will come from their inner circle of contacts but that they must quickly learn to generate ongoing appointments and referrals. Anyone can start a business with the support of friends and family members, but they won't sustain a business by relying on goodwill. Without ongoing appointments, they'll be out of business before their three-month anniversary, and you will have wasted all the work you put into sponsoring them.

This is the most critical area to monitor, so don't take your eye off the ball. Check in often to monitor how many appointments they have. If they're struggling to get appointments or bookings, the sooner you intervene the better your chances of refloating your sinking recruit. Once they run out of people to contact they will hit the bottom and you'll be facing a difficult salvage operation with only a slim chance of a recovery.

The more names they have on their contacts list the more people they will have to call. Use the "Who do I know?" prompter included in Chapter 8, and set the bar high by challenging them to list a hundred names in their first week.

Get your new distributors engaging on social media as soon as possible. It's no substitute for a personal call or visit, but it's an effective way to start spreading the word about their business. Start the ball rolling by posting a "Welcome to [company]" message on their newsfeed.

The more time your rookie distributors spend connecting with their contacts, the more likely it is their business will float. Not everyone will say yes, so prepare them to make lots of calls. As consistency is the key, set a target for them to contact ten prospects a day. You can share some simple tips to help them. Tell your rookies:

- You'll have better long-term results if you focus on renewing or strengthening your relationships, rather than trying to make a quick sale. Show an interest in what's new in their lives before you start talking about yourself.

- Keep the conversation light. This is not the time for a high-pressure business pitch.

- Don't worry about the "No's." Give your contacts a chance to say no.

- Don't let excitement cross the line into pressure. Give your friends time to think. Address their objections sensitively, and be gracious when you get a "No." No does not mean never.

- Accept that some appointments will come easily and others will take more effort. Stay positive, keep calling, and you'll get your appointments.

Try to instill good habits early. For example: "Schedule most of your appointments during the first three weeks of the month so you don't risk falling short of your monthly sales target and [lose your 5 percent bonus commission]. You can expect a few canceled or postponed appointments, but that becomes a problem only at the end of the month when you won't have time to schedule more in their place."

....

If you're in the party business, recommend that new distributors promote parties as the perfect excuse for a girls'-night-in. Keep the conversation light and talk about fun, friends, and free products. Suggest they send a picture of the current host incentive before they make the call with a message: "I have some of these to give away. Would you like one?"

....

STEP SEVEN: FOCUS ON THE NEW DISTRIBUTOR REWARDS TO DRIVE PERFORMANCE

Most companies have a new distributor reward program to focus rookies on the behaviors that will give their business the best possible start. Achieving these bonus rewards will boost their confidence, so promote them enthusiastically.

If they miss a reward, focus them immediately on the next one. Incentives can quickly become disincentives when new distributors fail to achieve them. Disappointment is one of the fastest paths out of the business.

STEP EIGHT: GET THEM WORKING AS SOON AND AS MUCH AS POSSIBLE, WHILE THEIR ADRENALINE LEVELS ARE HIGH

Practice makes perfect, and the only way to master the business is on the job. Remind rookies that their goal is sales, bookings, and new team members. If they talk about being nervous say: "A little stress is natural. It shows that you want to do a good job. The nerves will go away once you've made a few sales."

STEP NINE: TRACK THEIR FIRST APPOINTMENTS TO IDENTIFY STRENGTHS AND WEAKNESSES

Send a "good luck!" message before the first appointments, with an encouraging training tip if rookie distributors need it. Ask them to message their results to you, so you can monitor their progress. Make a follow-up call after as many appointments as possible, to give your new recruits feedback and guidance.

....

These simple text codes are a quick and effective way to get instant feedback on rookies' results before your follow-up coaching call.

The results of a party can be conveyed as 400 + 2 + 1 (meaning $400 sales, two bookings, and one business lead).

Yes is an appropriate code for a successful big-ticket item, subscription, or auto-ship sale.

....

STEP TEN: KEEP REFUELING THEIR EXCITEMENT AND SELF-ESTEEM

It can take only a few knocks to rattle a rookie's confidence. You can balance out the negatives with plenty of positive reinforcement. For example: "You're becoming a real asset to our team and our company. I'm confident that a few months from now you're going to tell me that this was one of the best decisions you ever made!"

Give honest feedback. You won't do your rookies any favors by giving them false praise or by reinforcing poor performance. For example: "You may not be progressing as fast as you want, but you're learning a lot and I admire your tenacity. The first few months are always the toughest so keep it up. You'll start getting results very soon, and what I suggest you do next is [tone your presentation down a little and focus on finding out what's happening in your prospects' life. They have to believe you have their best in-

terests in mind before they'll listen to what you're telling them]."
Feedback should always be specific and sincere.

Whatever happens, give your new recruits your time and attention during their first three months, and you will have the satisfaction of knowing you gave them their best possible chance of success.

CHAPTER 18

Chief Cheerleader: Celebrate *Everything*!

Every network marketing company places celebration high on its list of priorities. One of our key missions as an industry is to give our people the recognition and appreciation that they rarely get in their day-to-day lives.

From the welcome we extend to new distributors in our corporate news bulletins, to the electricity, excitement, and entertainment we generate at Convention, we seize every opportunity to celebrate. Some companies call their Conventions "Celebrations."

While you can't replicate the scale of corporate recognition, or the grandeur of a corporate event, you have the advantage of intimacy. You are close to your people. You know many, if not all of them personally. Seize every opportunity to let your team members know that they belong to a winning team with a leader who is rooting for their success. Shout your pride in your business, your company, your products, and your team members from the rooftops.

Appoint yourself "Chief Cheerleader" of your community and build celebration into your business strategy.

Host three social events every year. Kick-start the New Year with a "back to business" party, plan a midyear social event, and end the year with a celebration. A team that plays together stays together.

Dedicate specific months to celebrate the people who contribute to your business:

- Customer appreciation month
- Team appreciation month
- Host appreciation month
- Subscriber appreciation month
- Family appreciation month

Don't pass up opportunities to celebrate your team members' initiatives. Encourage them to share images of their product displays, market stall setups, promotional activities, and events.

Scatter photos showing your team members having fun at meetings and business and social events all over your team pages. Encourage them to post "selfies" on their way to, and during, Convention. Highlight as many team members as possible. No one wants to see the same faces over and over, and this is an opportunity to show your smaller performers they are valued.

Welcome everyone to meetings with a smile, handshake, or hug, as well as a "I'm glad you're here," "It's great to see you," or "Welcome back" greeting.

Recognize team members during their birthday month, anniversary month, or when they're celebrating *anything*! Make it fun. For example, buy a stack of oversized celebratory hats for them to wear throughout the meeting.

Seize any opportunity to laugh. Encourage everyone to share their business blunders at meetings and on Facebook. You'll also reveal a ton of funny incidents by inviting leaders to keep their ears and eyes open. An "Annual Blooper Awards" ceremony at your end-of-year meeting is guaranteed to become a highlight. Although your objective is to cultivate a sense of fun, celebrating mistakes and failures is a smart way to put them into perspective.

Don't tackle this important element of your business alone. Invite your liveliest team members to form a team celebration (or fun) committee to help you plan special events and recognition.

Openly and enthusiastically celebrate every achievement. Highlighting achievements bolsters everyone's belief in the business and focuses them on the actions that get results. There are countless ways to celebrate your team members' business achievements that will include contributors at all levels of involvement and status:

First order

First appointment

First party

First subscription or
   auto-ship customer

First ten subscription
   or auto-ship customers

Fifty active subscription
   or auto-ship customers

Ten appointments in
   first month

Six parties in first month

First recruit

Two recruits in first month

First out-of-state recruit

First international recruit

First second-level team
   member

Ten team members
   all levels

First $1,000 sales

First $5,000 sales

First $10,000 sales

First $50,000 sales

First $100,000 sales

Quarter million dollars
   lifetime sales

Half million dollars
   lifetime sales

Million dollars lifetime
   sales

First payday

First $1,000 payday

First $5,000 payday

First $10,000 payday

Active every month for
   six months

Active every month for
   full year

First quarter top sales

Second quarter top sales

Third quarter top sales

Fourth quarter top sales

First quarter top sponsoring

Second quarter top sponsoring

Third quarter top sponsoring

Fourth quarter top sponsoring

First time achieving personal sales bonus

First year "joining" anniversary

Achieved first month new distributor rewards

Achieved second month new distributor rewards

Achieved third month new distributor rewards

First title promotion

Subsequent title promotions

Maintain title first three months

Maintain title six months

Maintain title twelve months

Anniversary all title promotions

Promoted first leader

First Convention

Attended Convention every year since joining

Attended first team meeting

Attended all team meetings this year

Most consistent sales

Most consistent sponsoring

Top team sales

Top team sponsoring

Top ten team sales

Top ten team sponsoring

Top percentage team members active for month

First incentive trip

First to achieve incentive trip

Highest incentive trip achievement overall

Achieved company award

Booked first trade show or market

Ten trade shows in one year achiever

There's a reason cheerleaders are an integral part of a championship game, and why performers reserve front-row seats for their most dedicated fans. We feel stronger, reach higher, and try harder when surrounded by our strongest supporters. Become your team members' biggest fan, and let them feel it.

Network marketing leaders are intuitive and instinctive cheerleaders. They never miss an opportunity to celebrate their business, their team members, and the community they are privileged to lead.

CHAPTER 19

How to Motivate with Competition

Your most successful team members will almost always be highly competitive, and recognition and status will rank high among their goals. Talk to any high achievers about what motivates them, and you'll find these common themes emerge:

- I want to be number one!
- I want to walk across stage at next year's Convention!
- I want to prove to myself that I can do it!
- I want my family to see that I can be successful!

Healthy competition will bring out the best in your most ambitious team members, and those who seek to excel at everything they do.

Motivate your rising stars with encouraging messages:

- *I see huge potential in you.*
- *You definitely have leadership potential.*
- *Leadership is an opportunity you cannot afford to pass up.*

• *You can become a director before Convention if you want it.*

Run frequent team challenges. The most effective challenges are simple, short, and specific in their objective. For example, a twenty-four-hour booking blitz, or a three-day sponsoring challenge.
Before you launch a challenge consider:

• What result do I want to achieve (for example, a surge of activity at the start of a longer company incentive)?

• Can I tie the challenge to an existing company reward?

• What will the challenge be?

• What will the time frame be?

• How will I announce it?

• How will I inspire every team member to participate?

• How will I keep them energized, excited, and focused throughout the challenge?

• How will I recognize and/or reward those who meet the challenge?

Send congratulatory messages every time individual team members surpass a previous "personal best" result, and post "drum roll" messages on your team page to recognize achievers.
Pit your heavy hitters against each other in a spirit of friendly competition by introducing a BOBBYB (Beat Our Best Beat Your Best) challenge that recognizes team members who break team and personal records for sales or sponsoring. Keep your BOBBYB competition alive by running Lifetime Team Achiever leader boards.

Team members at any level can participate with their own BMB (Beat My Best) challenge. To participate, they simply track their all-time best sales month, sponsoring month, or highest sale from a one-on-one or group presentation for the satisfaction of beating it.

Spur on your most competitive team members by running "first past the post" challenges. For example, "first to achieve the incentive trip," "first to sponsor this month."

When two or more team members are running neck and neck for top achiever recognition in a month, encourage them to compete against each other. Although you must always take into account the personalities and dynamics between your frontrunners, sharing information about who's leading the pack toward the end of the month will bring out their competitive spirit.

Don't allow your star performers to become complacent. Feed them impromptu challenges during the last few days of the month to squeeze out more sales, or add another recruit.

Obviously you have to pick whom to motivate with challenges and competition. Not everyone is motivated by competition, but you will invariably find that your most determined people are. Let your knowledge of your team members' personalities and ambitions guide you as to whom to encourage with competitive challenges.

• •

One of the most powerful ways to encourage your highly driven team members is setting your personal activity bar high. When they see your name appearing on the company leader boards as a top achiever, they will be proud that they have a sponsor they can admire and emulate. Always lead from the front.

When I started my writing career I received this valuable advice from a best-selling author: "Publishers receive thousands of book submissions every week. Less than 1 percent has a chance of being published, and a fraction of those will sell more than a thousand copies. If you want to succeed, you have to compete with the top 1 percent."

When I am in danger of thinking, "This is good enough," I hear his voice saying, "Don't take your foot off the gas. You're competing with the best, not the rest."

It's a lesson that applies to any endeavor.

• •

Competition does not always need to be business related. Hosting a friendly weekend baseball or weeknight bowling tournament will bring out competitive spirit in your team members while doubling as an opportunity for socializing and networking.

Find ways to include your slow-but-steady performers in your recognition program. Consistent performers may not always earn the recognition they deserve unless you make a conscious effort to include them. Yet they are equally, if not more, deserving of recognition and will appreciate being acknowledged for their consistent contribution.

Remember that too much competition can demotivate less-competitive members, or those who are unable to compete because of circumstances. Always run your business with an attitude of gratitude and appreciation for every team member, however small his or her contribution may be.

PART FIVE

Going Forward

CHAPTER 20

Be a Great Conductor!

I vividly remember the first time I attended a live orchestral performance. I was awestruck that so many musicians, playing many different instruments, could produce such a flawless sound. I understood why the audience applauded enthusiastically when the concert concluded.

Only one thing puzzled me. When the conductor turned to take a bow, the applause lifted the roof. My awe had been directed at the musicians. To me the conductor had played the smallest role. He wasn't playing an instrument. How much talent does it take to wave a stick?

That was then. I now appreciate that the conductor creates the music. Regardless of how talented the performers are, the quality of the performance will be determined by how expertly the conductor elicits the best from each individual.

Become the conductor of your community. Whatever motivates your team members to join, or whatever ambitions or talents they bring to the team, learn to draw the maximum performance from each of them. Leaders who know how to harvest the potential that exists within every team member are always the most successful.

Many who join your community will be small producers. Some will stay small producers because they have modest aspirations, and others because they have other commitments. Only a few will have the desire, drive, and discipline to become star performers. Many of them won't show their star qualities at first.

Where it gets exciting is that many people will join with no thought of becoming leaders. Yet they will become leaders because you identified their potential, and used your skills and experiences to draw it out of them.

Never underestimate your power to move your team members beyond their self-doubts or comfort zones to become star performers. Every compensation plan reserves its highest rewards for those who develop leaders who develop leaders. Make it your mission to foster the potential that every member brings to the team.

Perhaps you were fortunate enough to have a mentor who played a pivotal role in your life. It may have been a teacher, church leader, sports coach, or scoutmaster who believed in you before you believed in yourself. It may have been a manager at your workplace who brought you out of your shell, or your sponsor who inspired you to reach higher, conquer your doubts, and overcome the limitations that stopped you from progressing. Many of us credit an inspiring, encouraging leader for giving us the confidence to grow, and a pathway to pursue.

I first became aware of the scope of the influence one person can have as a young student teacher. Our training included many school visits to gain classroom experience. It didn't take me long to notice that every school I visited had a distinct culture. It showed in the way I was greeted by the administrative staff at the main office and in how the teachers responded to a young student teacher whose presence added to their already heavy workload.

I saw it in the way the children engaged with each other on the playground, the teachers connected in the staff room, and the students and teachers interacted with each other in the classroom.

It had nothing to do with the location of the school. I worked in schools across a range of socioeconomic areas. It had everything to do with the example set by the head of the school. As goes the leader so goes the team.

I see the same phenomenon at every corporation I visit. The CEO's example has a direct and powerful influence on the morale and performance of staff at every level, from the receptionist to senior executives. There are no neutral leaders. A leader's influence is always positive or negative.

Do your own research and you'll see what a powerful influence one person can have on others. Observe the staff at your local retailers, restaurants, and businesses. Employees who are fortunate to have a focused, empathetic leader will be happier and more confident. They will be more accommodating and proactive as they interact with coworkers, service providers, and customers.

Many of network marketing's highest achievers started their businesses with small goals that exploded into huge goals after being inspired and encouraged by their sponsor or team leader.

Use your influence as the conductor of your community to inspire all team members to dream big dreams, and to keep working toward their goals no matter how many distractions or disappointments they must overcome. Let your positive, optimistic voice drown out the doubters and detractors and strengthen your team members' faith in the business and themselves.

Skilled conductors don't push every team member to perform all the time. Skilled conductors identify individual team members' talents, and the right time to encourage each one to shine. Some small performers may be bursting with potential and waiting for a chance to show their true colors. Others may be motivated to lift their game by a change in personal circumstances. When our situation changes, our goals can change in a heartbeat.

What makes this business exciting is that no matter what your team members' ambitions and talents are when they enter it, their opportunities are limitless. Their chances of success are greater if they have a purposeful, proactive leader who is dedicated to bringing out the best in every team member.

You'll always be a better conductor of your community if you monitor each team member's activity and results:

- Keep your team members focused on their most productive activities by encouraging them to make one-on-one and group presentations their core business.

- Advise them to view their personal calendars as the only accurate gauge of their businesses. Ask them to text or message you the appointments, parties, or presentations they have scheduled a week before every new month starts.

- Compare their appointments to the goals they set for themselves. A simple calculation will show you both how likely they are to exceed, meet, or fall short of their target when there's still time to generate more bookings.

- Encourage them to employ proactive strategies to meet their monthly sales target. For example, loading their calendars with bookings at the start of the month so that if an appointment cancels it can be rescheduled within the same month.

- Track active team members' schedules week by week so you can intervene if necessary with suggestions on how to make up for canceled or unproductive appointments.

Don't play dice with your overall business. Learn to evaluate its strength at the start of each month, and as the month evolves. If you leave it to the end of the month, it will be too late to take proactive action. Don't let inattention lead to a shortfall in results that will directly affect your income.

If you sell your product or service through one-on-one appointments, the most effective way to evaluate the strength of your month is to count appointments. For example:

- If you need $10,000 to reach your leadership status and rewards each month, and your average team sale is $1,000, you need ten teamwide sales. If on average your team converts one in three appointments into a sale,

you need a minimum of thirty appointments each
month, plus a few more to ensure against cancellations.

- If your business is party plan, the most effective way to
track your monthly target is to count parties. If you need
$10,000 to achieve and maintain your leadership status
and rewards and your average party sales total is $500,
your team must do approximately twenty parties.

Don't think minimums. If your average party is $500, base your
calculations on a more modest figure of $400. This will protect
your business from a shortfall caused by a run of cancellations or
lower than expected results.

When you step up as conductor of your community, you will
give every member a great shot at success. The impact your inspirational, influential leadership will have on your team will com-
pound. When we're among people who are energized, excited, and
motivated, we become more energized, excited, and motivated ourselves. As you bring out the best in each individual you'll move
your whole community toward performing at their peak.

CHAPTER 21

Embracing Change—
Your Competitive Edge

What's exciting about our industry is that we have always been at the forefront of innovation and change. While some industries resist change, network marketing has always been driven by change. We were among the first to:

- Take our products to our customers instead of expecting our customers to come to us.

- Offer our customers the convenience of seven-days-a-week, twenty-four-hours-a-day shopping.

- Work from a virtual office, from home, or on the go.

- Use our phones as remote controls for our businesses.

You can't avoid, ignore, or escape change. Your only option, unless you want your business to become fossilized, is to embrace it. Not some of it. All of it.

Think how excited you are when your company launches new products, packaging, or promotional materials. You're excited because they revitalize your brand, and give you the perfect excuse to excite and engage your customers.

No matter how much I love a product, if it's reformulated or discontinued it becomes a product I used to love. Clinging to products that have passed their use-by date isn't doing you or your customers any favors.

My favorite face cream has been replaced by a new formula? I have the perfect excuse to call my customers and say, "If you liked the old one, you are going to love the new one. It has been reformulated to [absorb deeper into your skin for longer-lasting benefits/give your skin a more luminescent glow]."

The bracelet I wear to all my shows has been discontinued? I will never wear it again. No one who compliments you on your jewelry wants to hear, "It's from last season's catalog and it's no longer available."

The insurance plan I sell to 90 percent of my clients has been replaced? I'm on the phone letting my clients know that I have good news. "The company has upgraded our most popular plans. When are you free this week so that I can pop in and show you why it's going to be better for you?"

Out with the old and in with the new. Change stops us falling into a rut and keeps our products and services from becoming stale.

> It is not the strongest of the species that survives,
> nor the most intelligent. It is the one that
> is most adaptable to change.
> UNKNOWN AUTHOR

It's equally important to accept changes the company makes to its programs, policies, or plan. Don't waste time questioning, or complaining about, company decisions. Even if you can't see the value, let it go.

Companies don't make changes on a whim. They know that changes can be unsettling, and they make them only with good reason:

- A stricter policy may be necessary to protect the majority of distributors from the questionable actions of a few.

- A compensation plan change may be necessary to distribute the rewards more equitably among active performers.

Any company that fails to innovate will quickly become out of touch and ill equipped to support its distributors. You may not like or agree with every change, but compromise is a component of any healthy partnership. Adjust your attitude from ignoring or fighting change to being excited and energized by change.

Instead of stressing about what you can't control, or complaining about tweaks to the business, think instead: How will I make the most of this change to grow my business? Missing, ignoring, or resisting change is a conscious act of business sabotage.

> How your team members embrace change is a measure of your leadership. As the conduit between your company and your team, it's your job to sell team members on the changes and address any concerns they have before they become a distraction. When you're discussing changes, always repeat and reinforce your message, "The company always has our best interests at heart."

Nowhere will change have more impact on your future income than in how you embrace a younger demographic. Millennials will fuel the next surge of network marketing, because they have the opportunity and the chutzpah to pursue a lifestyle their parents only fantasized about. Regardless of how old you are, you can't afford to miss out on the opportunity to ensure that your business has a steady flow of residual income in the future. Residual income is the reward you earn tomorrow for the work you do today.

If you were traveling to a new country, you would do some research to make the most of your experience. If you hope to enter millennial territory you must be willing to understand your future team members and leaders. Their perceptions have been shaped by completely different experiences. These steps will help enlighten you and let you have fun at the same time:

1. **Put Yourself in Their Shoes**

- Watch movies directed to a younger audience, to pick up words and phrases that young people use.

- Tune into television channels that target a younger audience and watch for differences in the content and delivery of programming and advertising.

- Sign up for promotional emails from companies that market to a younger demographic to observe differences in messaging and language.

- Listen to music by current artists.

- Frequent restaurants and stores that attract a younger crowd.

2. **Ask for Feedback**

- Show your catalog to younger friends and family members and ask them to tell you which products and messages they like.

- Share your opportunity brochure with younger people, and ask them to tell you what they respond to, and what they don't.

- If you don't understand something, ask for help. Young people are very willing to teach.

3. **Put Yourself in Front of Young People**

- Offer to speak to high school or college students on the pros and cons of owning your own business.

- Book booths at vendor events that target a younger market, and invite younger team members or friends to work the booth with you.

4. Change Your Messaging

- Don't be a digital dawdler. Millennials have lived only in a digital world, and you can't expect to interact effectively if you're reluctant to embrace new technologies. You don't have to be cool, but there's no excuse for being clueless.

  I often hear leaders complain: "I can't get my team to read my emails." Young people don't communicate by email. If you really, really want them to read an email, send a message saying, "I sent you an email."

- Make it about them. For example, instead of saying, "Our products are the best," try, "You'd make a great ambassador for our products."

- Ensure that your meetings and your conversations are high energy.

- Don't talk at them. They respond best to a more collaborative approach.

Above all, know your value. Young people expect to find a mentor who will give them the knowledge, encouragement, and recognition they need to get what they want. Offer to be that mentor.

Change is not something we do; it's what we are, and we will never stop evolving. What worked last year may not be enough to maintain your momentum next year. Your customers, prospects, and team members have never had so many choices, or such easy access to them. You have to be at the top of your game to earn their attention and their loyalty. A willingness to change will do more than ensure that your business survives. Keeping apace of change is how you will thrive.

No business can expect to succeed tomorrow by recycling yesterday's techniques. Millions of businesses close down every year, not because the owners stopped investing their time, effort, and energy into their businesses. They closed down because they were no longer relevant in today's changing market.

What gives you an edge is that you won't need to gain approval from a superior or consult a committee before you implement changes. You can make changes in seconds. And when it's not working, you can always try something new.

Don't be so busy working on your business that you miss the signals of change. Keep yourself plugged into the market. Listen to your customers. Check out your competitors. Go to conferences to learn about changes firsthand, and to understand why they are being implemented. Secondhand information is already stale by the time it reaches you.

Commit to learning something new every day. You can't keep pouring from an empty cup. Download company training calls to listen to when you're driving. Read books on network marketing, motivation, and leadership. A little often will yield better results than information overload, and so will putting what you learn into action. The magic of knowledge is in the application.

When you learn something new, think: *How will I apply this to my business?*

Just because you're in business for yourself doesn't mean you can excuse yourself from auditing your business every year. Results are the only true gauge of your performance, and by conducting annual reviews you can evaluate what's working for you and what needs to change:

- Did my personal sales grow?
- Did my personal team grow?
- Did our team sales grow?
- Did our team sponsor more people?
- Did we keep more people?
- Did more team members come to Convention?
- Did more team members achieve the incentive trip?
- Did we promote leaders?
- Are more team members coming to meetings?

- Are more team members participating in calls and webinars?

- Are my team members actively engaged on Facebook?

- Are there any cracks in team morale?

- Are there any unresolved issues that need to be addressed?

- How healthy are my relationships with my sponsor, up-line leaders, and corporate staff?

- Are my team members more confident, positive, and optimistic about the business?

- Am I more confident, positive, and optimistic about the business?

Your business is either growing or it's slipping, and if you're not proactively looking for ways to improve, you'll always be vulnerable to shifting market conditions.

Leaders never stop learning and never stop growing. They're on a continual quest for personal improvement and they never stop questioning:

- What do I need to stop doing?

- What do I need to start doing?

- What do I need to do differently?

- What do I need to do *now*?

....

The Power of Innovation

Dr. Traci Lynn, founder, Traci Lynn Jewelry

Creativity is *thinking up new things.* Innovation *is doing new things.*

THEODORE LEVITT

As an evolving, growing, breathing business, network marketing thrives on innovation. If we don't innovate we will become dinosaurs . . . extinct!

Learning to innovate means being willing to take risks. If you don't take risks you will always work for someone who does. You are stronger than you think, so trust your intuition and never let fear of change prevent you from being innovative.

One of our emerging leaders was a skilled recruiter who consistently recruited ten people a month. Then she realized that more than half were gone within ninety days. She refused to accept these statistics, because she believed in our company philosophy—*The System Works & The System Pays Me!*

Instead of being discouraged by how many people were leaving, she seized it as an opportunity to be innovative. Along with another leader she developed a program for new recruits called *Let's Go into the Lab*. The program focused on personal development, business development, and company culture.

The results were astounding. After implementing the program they started retaining up to 80 percent of all their new recruits. The initiative was so successful we adopted the curriculum at the corporate level so that every leader could benefit.

What was important is that she was able to measure the success of her program. For many leaders, coming up with ideas isn't the problem. The challenge is to turn good ideas into initiatives that make a measurable impact.

Three years ago our company took a bold step that some may classify as a huge risk. But after analyzing our results we realized that if we didn't make changes we would not be able to take care of our people.

We moved our corporate office from Delaware to Ft. Lauderdale, taking only two of our twenty employees, and building a new corporate team. We revamped our catalog and developed new products. Each move was risky in itself, but collectively they added up to a huge risk. Even though we made calculated decisions, our changes quickly swirled into a storm.

Major software problems meant that we could not process new consultant kits. Most new recruits who signed up during this time canceled.

But even with the resulting loss of revenue we did not lose our way. We knew that innovation doesn't come without risk, so we hoisted the sail up a little higher and became more resilient, focused, and determined than ever before. We believed that if we didn't make changes we would not be able to stay competitive. The destiny of our people was at stake.

After the storm subsided, there was debris everywhere, but before year end we were able to make up for all that was lost. Over the last few years we have seen phenomenal growth, advancement, and innovation in new areas, proof that we made the right move.

Creating a culture of change takes a willingness to relinquish control. You have to be confident enough to lead your business but not control it. Your people will embrace your innovations when they believe that you always have their best interests at heart.

Imagination is everything.
It is the preview of life's coming attractions.
ALBERT EINSTEIN

Conclusion

Never doubt that you have what it takes to lead a profitable network marketing empire. You became a leader the day you signed your independent contractor agreement. Don't wait until you have a team before you start thinking of yourself as a leader, and acting as a leader. The sooner your attitudes and actions align with the attitudes and actions of a leader, the sooner your community will grow.

Leading a community is a big responsibility, but don't let that overwhelm you. Let it inspire you to be the best leader you can be.

No one is more worthy or more deserving of success than you. Your success will not come at the cost of someone else's success. You won't have to play politics, deal with bullying bosses, or go head-to-head with your colleagues to win the highest-paying jobs. As I said at the start, we all get to run our own race.

People reach the top of network marketing from every direction in life. We are teachers, engineers, accountants, and artists. We are students, veterans, moms, and dads. What draws us to network marketing is a better life.

Network marketing has lifted our families out of debt, funded our children's college educations, built our dream homes, and paid for our luxury vacations. It has made a profound difference to families hit by layoffs and job losses, and allowed millions of children to have a stay-at-home parent without their family scraping by on one income.

What brought us into the business is not why we stay. Our goals tend to expand as our businesses gain traction. So does our influence. The only way we achieve what we want is by helping others achieve what they want.

The measure of your success will be your paycheck. But if you sincerely care about helping others, your vision for your business will be more than a whopping payday. It will be that every community member's life is enriched for having you in it, no matter how long they stay or what they achieve.

Build your community with empathy, integrity, and authenticity. No amount of money or recognition will surpass the satisfaction you'll feel knowing you made a difference in other people's lives.

As you grow your business you'll make mistakes. You'll face challenges that are beyond your control, and some of them will come at you without warning. But they'll only stop you if you choose to see them as insurmountable. I have never met a leader who had a smooth ride to the top, only leaders who were willing to change gears as conditions dictated.

If your business slows or stalls only you can get it back on track. Don't waste time hoping for something to change, or looking for someone to blame. Keep your focus and your energy directed on how you will change. Above all, be prepared to ask yourself the tough questions:

- Am I allowing self-doubt to come between me and my dreams?
- Am I worrying about things outside my control?
- Am I easily distracted by what others think?
- Am I wasting time on unimportant stuff?
- Am I reluctant to embrace change?

- Am I wallowing in what's wrong rather than what's right?
- Am I blaming others for my failures?
- Am I doing enough?
- Am I making the right moves?

Leaders don't let self-doubt determine their path in life. If you don't believe you deserve a fulfilling life you'll always be pushing uphill to achieve it. No barrier between you and your goal will be unmovable if your faith in yourself is unshakable.

As your community grows you'll discover strengths you never knew existed. You'll enrich your life, and the lives of your loved ones. You'll discover that there's no limit to how many lives you can change.

The only casualties of this business are those who let fear stop them from taking bold steps, or who let a temporary failure become a permanent disability. Network marketing can be a tough teacher. You'll often get the test first and the lesson after.

When I first moved to America I lived in Los Angeles. Los Angeles has a reputation as a city of dreamers. I saw it differently. In my eyes, every aspiring actor waiting tables or working a low-paid retail job while spending every spare moment taking acting classes, or standing in an audition line, was a doer. Every actor sleeping on a friend's couch, so she could spend every dollar she earned on voice or dance lessons, was a doer, not a dreamer. They were doers because they were willing to take whatever steps were necessary to pursue their dreams.

I remember the bright-eyed server who couldn't hold back from sharing, "I just got a part in *CSI*"; the salon assistant now working in the special effects department of a movie production company; the young man whose first job in Hollywood was making coffee, and whose name now appears on the screen credits as executive director on two prime-time shows.

Not everyone will succeed. It's the same in any endeavor. Not everyone who goes to college graduates, or lands his dream job. Only a percentage of those who get a job will ever reach the executive floor. A fraction of aspiring singers and writers will become household names. But I applaud them all. All I say to those who sneer is: "Please don't trample on their dreams."

It's true that only a small percentage of those who start a network marketing business will achieve a six-figure income. But before you ask, "Why me?" stop and ask, "Why not me?"

To succeed you must close your ears to those who seek to make themselves feel better by making you feel worse. Pursue your dreams and let karma take care of the doubters.

When you lose your fear of failure, and cut loose from the expectations and opinions of others, you free yourself to pursue what you want in life.

> It's lovely to know the world can't
> interfere with the inside of your head.
> FRANK McCOURT

Success is a journey you take one step at a time. There may be many twists, troughs, and turbulence on the path between you and your goal. But if your goal is big enough you'll never get lost. Its glow will eclipse anything your journey throws at you.

Hold on tight to your dreams. No matter what it takes, keep moving toward them. It takes courage, not confidence, to pursue the life you dream about, and you'll fail only if you quit before you succeed.

> As we let our own light shine, we unconsciously
> give other people permission to do the same.
> MARIANNE WILLIAMSON

Top Twenty Direct Sales Countries by Sales in U.S. Dollars (Estimated)

Country	U.S. Dollars (billions)	Country	U.S. Dollars (billions)
1. United States	32.7	11. United Kingdom	3.3
2. China	27.3	12. Colombia	3.3
3. Japan	17.9	13. Taiwan	3.1
4. Korea	14.5	14. Italy	3.1
5. Brazil	14.2	15. Thailand	3.0
6. Germany	8.6	16. Canada	2.0
7. Mexico	8.1	17. Argentina	1.9
8. France	5.3	18. Peru	1.9
9. Malaysia	4.7	19. Australia	1.4
10. Russia	4.3	20. Venezuela	1.4

Top Twenty Countries with Highest Percentage Annual Growth

Country	Percentage	Country	Percentage
1. China	41.0%	11. Taiwan	6.4%
2. Argentina	38.0%	12. Peru	5.7%
3. Venezuela	15.0%	13. Germany	4.2%
4. Indonesia	15.0%	14. France	3.9%
5. Philippines	14.8%	15. United States	3.3%
6. India	11.7%	16. Korea	2.9%
7. Mexico	8.5%	17. Russia	2.7%
8. Brazil	7.2%	18. Australia	2.3%
9. United Kingdom	6.7%	19. Thailand	1.9%
10. Colombia	6.7%	20. Malaysia	1.8%

Top Fifty Network Marketing Companies Worldwide

This data collected by the World Federation of Direct Selling Associations (WFDSA) of the top fifty companies worldwide (by net sales) is not intended as a recommendation. Its purpose is to show you the diversity of products and services that are available through network marketing channels.

Your opportunities for advancement will be similar whether you choose to join a brand new start-up company, or a globally established brand. One of the keys to your success will be finding a company whose products or services you are passionate about.

#1 Amway USA
Sales Method: Person-to-person
Compensation Structure: Multi-level
Products: Cosmetics, personal care, food and beverage, home décor, kitchenware and appliances, home care, wellness

#2 Avon Products Inc. USA
Sales Method: Person-to-person
Compensation Structure: Multi-level
Products: Cosmetics, personal care, clothing and accessories, home décor, kitchenware and appliances

#3 Herbalife Ltd. USA
Sales Method: Person-to-person
Compensation Structure: Multi-level
Products: Cosmetics, personal care, wellness

#4 Mary Kay Inc. USA
Sales Method: Person-to-person and party plan
Compensation Structure: Single-level
Products: Cosmetics, personal care

#5 Vorwerk & Co. KG Germany
Sales Method: Person-to-person and party plan
Compensation Structure: Multi-level
Products: Cosmetics, household appliances, home care

#6 Natura Cosméticos SA Brazil
Sales Method: Person-to-person
Compensation Structure: Multi-level
Products: Cosmetics, personal care

#7 Infinitus China
Sales Method: Person-to-person
Compensation Structure: N/A
Products: Health care

#8 Tupperware Brands Corp. USA
Sales Method: Person-to-person and party plan
Compensation Structure: Single-level and multi-level
Products: Storage and serving, beauty, personal care

#9 Nu Skin Enterprises Inc. USA
Sales Method: Person-to-person
Compensation Structure: Multi-level
Products: Cosmetics, personal care, wellness

#10 JoyMain China
Sales Method: Person-to-person
Compensation Structure: N/A
Products: Nutrition, health care, home care, clothing

#11 Oriflame Cosmetics SA Luxembourg
Sales Method: Person-to-person
Compensation Structure: Multi-level
Products: Cosmetics, personal care

#12 Ambit Energy USA
Sales Method: Person-to-person
Compensation Structure: Multi-level
Products: Energy

#13 Belcorp Ltd. Peru
Sales Method: Person-to-person and party plan
Compensation Structure: Single-level and multi-level
Products: Cosmetics, personal care

#14 Primerica Inc. USA
Sales Method: Person-to-person
Compensation Structure: Multi-level
Products: Financial services

#15 Tiens China
Sales Method: Person-to-person
Compensation Structure: Single-level
Products: Health care

#16 Telecom Plus UK
Sales Method: Person-to-person
Compensation Structure: Multi-level
Products: Landline phones, broadband, mobile phones, gas, electricity, cash back cards

#17 New Era Healthy Industry Group (Zhong Jian) China
Sales Method: Person-to-person
Compensation Structure: Single-level
Products: Health care, cosmetics, cleaning

#18 Stream Energy USA
Sales Method: Person-to-person
Compensation Structure: Multi-level
Products: Energy and home life services

#19 Miki Corp. Japan
Sales Method: Not available
Compensation Structure: Not available
Products: Food, cosmetics, household products

#20 Yanbal International Peru
Sales Method: Person-to-person
Compensation Structure: Multi-level
Products: Cosmetics, personal care, skin care, jewelry, fragrances

#21 Shaklee USA
Sales Method: Person-to-person
Compensation Structure: Multi-level
Products: Nutritional supplements, skin care, weight management, green cleaners

#22 ACN Inc. USA
Sales Method: Person-to-person
Compensation Structure: Multi-level
Products: Telecommunications, energy

#23 Pola Japan
Sales Method: Person-to-person
Compensation Structure: Single-level
Products: Cosmetics, skin care, personal care, nutrition

#24 USANA Health Sciences Inc. USA
Sales Method: Person-to-person
Compensation Structure: Multi-level
Products: Wellness

#25 DXN Holdings BHD Malaysia
Sales Method: Person-to-person
Compensation Structure: Multi-level
Products: Cosmetics, personal care, food and beverage, home care, wellness

#26 Cosway Corp. Ltd. Malaysia
Sales Method: Person-to-person
Compensation Structure: Not available
Products: Supplements, skin care, personal care, cosmetics, household products, car care, food and beverage, clothing

#27 Isagenix Worldwide LLC USA
Sales Method: Person-to-person
Compensation Structure: Multi-level
Products: Wellness

#28 Thirty-One Gifts USA
Sales Method: Party plan and group sales
Compensation Structure: Multi-level
Products: Handbags, totes

#29 Market America Inc. USA
Sales Method: Person-to-person
Compensation Structure: Single-level
Products: Cosmetics, personal care, food and beverage, home care, leisure and educational, services, wellness

#30 Noevir Co. Ltd. Japan
Sales Method: Person-to-person
Compensation Structure: Single-level
Products: Skin care, body care,
  nutritional supplements, cosmetics

#31 For You China
Sales Method: Person-to-person
Compensation Structure: N/A
Products: Cosmetics, health care,
  personal care, home care, food
  and beverage

#32 It Works! Global USA
Sales Method: Person-to-person
Compensation Structure: Multi-level
Products: Cosmetics, personal care,
  wellness

#33 Team Beachbody USA
Sales Method: Person-to-person
Compensation Structure: Multi-level
Products: Wellness

#34 Rolmex China
Sales Method: Person-to-person
Compensation Structure: N/A
Products: Cosmetics, nutritional
  supplements

#35 Forbes Lux Group Switzerland
  & India
Sales Method: Person-to-person,
  person-to-business
Compensation Structure: Single-level
Products: Water and air purifiers, home
  and professional cleaning systems,
  electronic security solutions

#36 AdvoCare International LP USA
Sales Method: Person-to-person
Compensation Structure: Multi-level
Products: Wellness

#37 Arbonne International LLC USA
Sales Method: Person-to-person
Compensation Structure: Multi-level
Products: Cosmetics, personal care,
  wellness

#38 Apollo (Taiyang Shen) China
Sales Method: Person-to-person
Compensation Structure: Single-level
Products: Nutritional drinks

#39 Jeunesse Global USA
  (Tied with Scentsy Inc. USA)
Sales Method: Person-to-person
Compensation Structure: Multi-level
Products: Cosmetics, personal care,
  wellness

#39 Scentsy Inc. USA
  (Tied with Jeunesse Global USA)
Sales Method: Party plan and
  group sales
Compensation Structure: Multi-level
Products: Accessories, food and
  beverage, home décor, kitchenware
  and appliances

#40 Nerium International USA
Sales Method: Party plan and
  group sales
Compensation Structure: Multi-level
Products: Cosmetics, personal care

#41 YOFOTO (China) Health Industry Co. Ltd. China
Sales Method: Person-to-person
Compensation Structure: Multi-level
Products: Wellness

#42 Team National Inc. USA
Sales Method: Person-to-person
Compensation Structure: Multi-level
Products: Clothing and accessories, cosmetics and personal care, food and beverage, home décor, kitchenware and appliances, services, wellness

#43 Nature's Sunshine Products Inc. USA
Sales Method: Person-to-person
Compensation Structure: Multi-level
Products: Botanicals, dietary supplements, skin care, general wellness

#44 KK ASSURAN Japan
Sales Method: Person-to-person
Compensation Structure: Multi-level
Products: Skin care

#45 For Days Co. Ltd. Japan
Sales Method: Person-to-person
Compensation Structure: Single-level
Products: Personal care, cosmetics

#46 WorldVentures USA
Sales Method: Person-to-person
Compensation Structure: Multi-level
Products: Travel packages

#47 PartyLite USA
Sales Method: Party plan
Compensation Structure: Multi-level
Products: Candles, fragrance, home décor

#48 4Life Research LLC USA
Sales Method: Person-to-person
Compensation Structure: Multi-level
Products: Wellness

#49 Rodan + Fields Dermatologists USA
Sales Method: Person-to-person
Compensation Structure: Multi-level
Products: Cosmetics, personal care

#50 Viridian Energy USA
Sales Method: Person-to-person
Compensation Structure: Multi-level
Products: Energy

Source: *World Federation of Direct Selling Associations Report 2014.*

Index

About the Author

Mary Christensen is one of the most successful and respected leaders in direct selling. Not surprisingly, she is one of direct selling's most sought-after speakers worldwide. Her bestselling books *Be a Direct Selling Superstar*, *Be a Recruiting Superstar*, *Be a Party Plan Superstar*, and *Be a Network Marketing Superstar* are published in many languages, including Spanish and French, and all are available in print, ebook, and audio formats.

Mary has walked the talk in all aspects of direct sales, including as an independent contractor, former CEO of two direct selling corporations, and a past president of the Direct Selling Association (NZ). In 2013 when she entered a new market, Australia, three thousand consultants signed on and fifty were promoted to leader within the first ten months.

Direct Selling Live named Mary one of the ten most influential women in direct selling worldwide, and the Multi-Level Marketing International Association honored Mary as recipient of its Best of the Best Worldwide award.

MARY CHRISTENSEN'S OTHER BOOK TITLES

Be a Direct Selling Superstar will guide you step-by-step through how to build, lead, and manage a six-figure-income business.

Be a Recruiting Superstar is your "go-to" guide for identifying, approaching, and sponsoring new team members.

Be a Network Marketing Superstar is the perfect book for distributors who are starting out, or rebuilding an existing business.

Be a Party Plan Superstar is full of tips and techniques for party planners.